I Believe, I Doubt

D1368971

I Believe, I Doubt

Notes on Christian Experience

Günther Weber

SCM PRESS LTD

Translated by John Bowden from the German *Ich glaube, ich zweifle, Notizen im nachhinein,* published 1996 by Benziger Verlag, Zurich and Düsseldorf

© Benziger Verlag 1996

Translation © John Bowden 1998

All rights reserved. No part of this publication may be reproduced, stored in a retrieval system, or transmitted, in any form or by any means, electronic, mechanical, photocopying or otherwise, without the prior permission of the publisher, SCM Press Ltd.

0 334 02742 X

First published 1998 by
SCM Press Ltd
9-17 St Albans Place London N1 0NX

Typeset by Regent Typesetting, London
Printed in Great Britain by
Biddles Ltd, Guildford and King's Lynn

Contents

Contents   xi

Contents

I believe – I doubt

I believe

Even now, with advancing years, I stand by the decision which I first made in my youth: the decision for Christian faith, the decision to take Jesus Christ, the person who stands at the centre of this faith, as the basic guide for my life and thought, my questions and my action.

I believe that in the life and teaching of Jesus a 'truth' has come to light which can guide my basic attitude to the world and human life, and also shape my relationship to the fundamental mystery of existence that we call God. I believe that this man from Nazareth lived in deep harmony with God and that therefore he can show men and women a way to a more human, a fuller life.

I also believe that even after the death of this Jesus, a spirit emanates from him which over the ages can seize people, change them and make them better. I believe that this spirit, the spirit of God, can bind together people who become open to it in a fellowship which we call church. So I still count myself a member of this fellowship, despite everything in the church that seems to me to be questionable.

All my life and thought has been guided by this faith. It has preoccupied me a great deal in my thinking and questioning and has made an essential mark on my career and some of my personal decisions. I have grown up with it; one could almost say that I am 'indissolubly' tied to it.

I still say 'Yes' to Christian faith even today.

I doubt

But I must also honestly confess that despite all my ties to the Christian faith and to the church, in the background my faith has always also been accompanied by doubts, sometimes greater and sometimes less. I don't deny it. The doubts certainly did not arise from any basic repudiation of faith or the church. On the contrary, they grew out of a concern to be responsible for my faith and by thinking to get closer to what it means.

The doubts which accompanied and often oppressed my faith have been 'suffered through' – I am almost embarrassed to put this so pretentiously. So they are important, at least for me. Now that I am older, in retrospect they oppress me more strongly than before. Perhaps that is also because in the 'freedom' which old age grants I can ask, reflect and speak more openly.

Should I now simply suppress the doubts which thrust themselves on me? Should I put them on one side? Can I keep an unquestioned certainty of faith in this way? Or should I – like so many people who teach or write in the church – conceal my doubts, keep them to myself, suppress them or mask them? That would probably have been wiser and would perhaps spare me a good deal of trouble.

But does this repression and silencing of critical thoughts do justice to the claim of faith? Like faith, doubts too have a right to be taken seriously. They too have a right to be faced, expressed and identified, questioned and thought through, so that faith is truthful. For these doubts have grown out of the same ground in which I once recognized Christian faith: the quest for truth.

Doubting – part of discovering the truth

In the language of the church the word 'doubt' does not have good connotations, especially if it is used in conjunction with the word 'believe'. Here doubting always appears as a thoroughly destructive process which endangers faith and puts it in question.

Faith and doubt seem to be mutually exclusive. Those who truly believe, deeply and firmly, know no doubts. And those who have doubts do not have a strong faith. Doubting is dangerous for belief: it can threaten it and destroy it. Doubt is thought to be directed against God, against faith and against the church, and therefore is rejected and even regarded as sinful. We still read in the papal Catechism of 1993: 'Voluntary doubt about the faith disregards or refuses to hold as true what God has revealed and the Church proposes for belief' (1/ no.2087).

But is it really right to judge doubt in such a one-sidedly negative way? Is doubt really the hostile counterpart to faith? Only those who seek a truth really have doubts. That already begins in ordinary everyday life, when we ask whether what we have been told is really true and whether we can rely on it, or when we consider whether our previous thoughts were really right, or perhaps need to be corrected on the basis of new information.

In the realm of scholarly thought – from Socrates through Descartes to Karl Popper – doubt is regarded as an indispensable element in the discovery of truth and the formation of knowledge. Almost all important new discoveries which have led to deeper insights into situations and to a greater approximation of knowledge to truth came about because doubts emerged over the correctness and validity of existing opinions and teachings. And once these doubts emerged, they became the foundation for a new understanding which pointed towards the future.

So as a matter of course the sciences take it for granted that their answers are only provisional and need to be corrected as soon as new insights require this. Therefore in contrast to religious faith they guarantee freedom to doubt the results that have been discovered.

Doubting in faith

Now religious faith and scientific knowledge are not the same thing. Faith approaches the 'object' of its knowledge and language, the basic mystery of being, called God, in a different way from the sciences. Christian faith appeals to a historical communication from God, to a revelation.

However, the 'truth' which dawned on biblical men and women, especially in their encounter with the person, the life and the teaching of Jesus, is not simply identical with the understanding which has found expression in the statements and doctrines with which the church tradition has attempted for almost two thousand years to grasp, maintain, express and communicate this 'truth' with understanding. Like all other human knowledge, understanding and speech, knowledge, understanding and speech in the sphere of faith are limited by the possibilities of human knowledge and its attachment to time-conditioned ideas. Church history proves this.

In the course of my life I have learned to be sceptical about my own certainty that I have recognized something to be right and true. I have had to correct myself too often. So I have also learned to be sceptical about others who claim on the basis of their position or on the basis of a tradition to possess truth which is free from error. Doubt in the final validity and immutability of a given understanding of faith represents a humble recognition of the limitations of human understanding, from which even the believer is not exempt. Constant new enquiry keeps one's eyes open to the dimension of that truth transcending all knowledge to which faith refers. There is not only a 'doubting in faith' but also a 'doubting as a result of faith'.

If I did not believe, questions about the truth of faith would not oppress me so. If I did not allow myself to be oppressed by questions about the truth of faith, I would not have come to doubt. If I did not believe and doubt, I would not have written these notes.

Believing – more than regarding something as true

Believing in the biblical sense, above all believing as Jesus understood it, is a trusting and bold reliance on that ultimate reality
which Jesus calls 'Father'. This faith is always more than
unchallenged orthodoxy. Faith is always more than obedient
and passive belief in the truth of a catalogue of convictions presented by a faith community.

Anyone who is satisfied with a faith which takes the form of
uncritical assent to the truth of the doctrines presented by an
infallible hierarchy will hardly be oppressed with doubts. The
truth is in fact already there. One only needs to take it over 'in
the obedience of faith'. And the less one asks and reflects, the
less problematical this will prove.

But anyone who wants not just to share in the faith handed
down by the church, but also to affirm it thoughtfully and be
intellectually responsible, will necessarily be led into a dis-
cussion which raises critical questions. And in so doing he or
she will also come to know doubt. The doubt which seeks truth
is part of an intellectually responsible, mature faith.

Doubt is the critically alert companion of faith, not its enemy.
Even in faith, doubt helps us to seek, find and preserve the truth.
Without constant critical questions, faith is in danger of
degenerating into a museum piece, hardening into authoritarian
doctrine or degenerating into superstition. A faith which avoids
doubt in the long term also avoids the claim of its own truth; it
loses its credibility.

The centuries-long self-confident and arrogant rejection of
all the doubts announced by the Enlightenment and modern
science has opened up an almost unbridgeable gulf between
present-day human thought and the statements of the church's
magisterium. More and more people do not know what to make
of the so-called truths which the church asks them to believe.
And so they turn their backs on the church.

Doubt does not sustain us

Doubt is not a pleasant companion. Those who entrust themselves solely to its guidance soon go through barren land. No
flowers blossom by the wayside. And quite often the wilderness
waits at the end of the journey. Nor is doubt as certain of itself
as it claims to be. I never completely trust it, and I do not hand
myself over to it, even if I take it seriously. I remain sceptical
about doubt also.

Doubt alone cannot answer any of the urgent questions of
human existence. It recognizes the cracks in the plastered walls
of the old house; it discovers the crumbling foundations below
it. It can pull down a house, but it cannot build a new one.
Often it leaves behind only emptiness. And mourning! It does
not give us a home; it does not offer us any support. It does not
warm us; it leaves us cold. The heart finds no abode in the land
of doubt.

Doubt does not give us any bread; it leaves us hungry.
Perhaps it is doubt in particular that keeps making the heart
search anew for a faith which can satisfy its hunger for truth,
for a faith which will also withstand critical questions.

The 'notes' in this book are an expression of this quest.

Remaining certain?

It is easy to understand how even believers who think critically
and seek the truth are constantly inclined to repress dawning
doubts. They do not want to endanger their faith, which also
gives them certainty in life. They all too readily refuse to engage
in thinking which could put in question the accustomed ways of
religious thought and behaviour. Contradictions are smoothed
over and inconsistencies concealed, preferably not noted at all.
Critical objections are repudiated almost instinctively, often
very emotionally.

Psychological and sociological factors influence perception

and knowledge, thought and evaluation. Some obstacles and blocks to thought, knowledge and understanding are not grounded in people's intelligence and knowledge but have their roots in the depths of their make-up, their situations, their biography and their social relationships. There is an unconscious selection of information: some is accepted and assimilated, or not even taken account of in the first place.

To put in question convictions which are deeply rooted in the structure of one's life and have been supportive often means putting in question all one's previous certainties, everything which gave meaning to life. This leads to a fear of dropping out of the group in which one is intellectually and socially at home, losing its acceptance and its good will, and becoming isolated.

The temptation to reject doubts is especially great among those who are deeply involved in church life, and may even have an office or a function. Over a long period I too was constantly inclined to protect my faith in a similar way and to fight shy of thoughts which caused doubts.

But can one really preserve a certainty of faith in this way?

Is a faith which has to preserve itself by repressing and warding off questions which seek the truth really still faith as Jesus understood it?

Why I repressed doubt

For many years I was engaged in the task of proclaiming the Christian faith. I wrote books on religious education, gave lectures and reports at hundreds of conferences, and even had a senior and responsible church position in religious education, its theory and practice. I often ask myself how, over these years, I did not see the many improbable and incredible features in church doctrines and so seldom began to doubt.

During them, my intellectual efforts had been predominantly directed towards understanding and appropriating the church's tradition of faith. I was concerned to reflect on what the church tradition had already thought out, and only rarely did I find the courage to investigate a particular matter for myself, to develop my own understanding. Somehow my thought was paralysed. How can a single individual put in question doctrines which have been handed down in a two-thousand-year history of faith, a process in which the greatest minds of the West were involved, a process which moreover was guided by the Holy Spirit?

When some doctrines nevertheless seemed hardly credible to me, I usually sought the cause of this in myself: in my defective knowledge and in an insufficiently deep understanding, even in a lack of humility which prevented me from accepting the principles of the church's faith without understanding them or assenting to them with my mind. I would doubt myself rather than doubt the doctrines of the church.

Certainly even then I found individual church doctrines quite incredible and doubtful, but at the time I didn't attach much importance to my doubts. Somehow I felt that only a few doctrines were incredible. They did not disturb my faith, because basically my faith was not rooted in the church as an institution or in a system of doctrines or in individual accounts in the Bible, but in a personal relationship to Jesus.

So what the church said about faith seemed to me to be secondary. Its statements were historically conditioned and always imperfect attempts by believers, mostly from centuries long past, to understand their personal acts of faith and put them into words. They could do this only in the ideas current in their time. And these were quite different from those of today.

More recent scholarly theology helped me to recognize the historical character of church doctrines and to distinguish their abiding core of truth from their historical garb. This enabled me to say my creed of traditional faith while seeking truth in my thinking. I fervently hoped that it was only a matter of time before a more up-to-date understanding of the Christian faith was established in the church, which could also make it possible for thinking people today to assent to the faith.

However, later it became clear to me that my hope was in

vain, when Pope John Paul II began to impress the stamp of his clericalistic spirituality and his dogmatic traditionalism on the church.

Then I seriously began to have doubts.

Not pulling down the house

It is not the Christian faith itself which I find questionable, nor belief in Jesus and his teaching.

What I find questionable are the language of doctrine, the traditional forms of thought and language which the church tends to use to explain, express and describe its faith. Because they come from other periods of history, rather than disclosing the truth of faith and shedding light on it, for me, and probably for many, many other people who want to believe, they conceal and distort it.

In the following 'notes', I want to attempt with the utmost personal truthfulness and honesty to ask my way through the obstacles which make it so difficult for me to believe with intellectual honesty in so many doctrines which the church asks me to believe. Perhaps the personal understanding of traditional truths of faith which I have arrived at here and now may also help others still to be believing Christians in the church today and tomorrow.

I do not want to pull down the house in which I have lived and worked for so long, and which is the home of so many friends and people whom I respect. On the contrary, my questions about the truth of church doctrines are so insistent because I want to find some firm ground on which I can build: ground which does not give way if I burden it with thoughts.

Searching

Many people who speak and write in the church sphere attempt to remove difficulties by disguising or even keeping quiet about thoughts which deviate from the predominant official church understanding. That is why church statements are usually so woolly, selective, sterile and empty. In these 'notes' I want to attempt to write down openly and honestly what is not contradicted by the present state of my knowledge.

The 'notes' document a search for understanding; they do not offer any finished answers. I feel that I can seek a new personal understanding of traditional religious notions, even if it should be rather different from the way in which they are traditionally understood in the church.

Fundamental trust comes through the Bible

The old scholastic statement that all that is true, good and beautiful comes together in God is still important for me. I believe that to seek truth and to seek God is the same thing. An approach to God is involved in any approach to truth. So I can openly and critically investigate my doubts. My questions and thought have their foundation in the fundamental trust that comes to me through the Bible. I can never lose God if I seek truth, even if in the process some vessels in which past generations once attempted to contain and preserve truth get broken.

A God whom I lost because I pestered him with too many questions in an honest search for truth could not have been God. What I had regarded as God would have been an idol: an idol clothed with the imposing garments of 'infallible' doctrine. If I stopped constantly investigating the ground and truth of faith, I would feel that I had given up the quest for that God who *is* the truth.

Biblical faith began with Abraham, a man who set out from the well-ordered security of his familiar world, and ventured into the unknown to seek a new land. He trusted that the God who said to him 'Set out!' was with him. So I trust that in asking questions in search of the truth I shall not fall into an abyss, but come upon a foundation which can again support my faith in a changed form.

All life must keep leaving its old forms behind and changing, so that it can survive in a new form. Otherwise it ceases to be alive.

It is just the same with faith.

2

God no longer enthroned in heaven

Beliefs – dependent on our picture of the world?

Biblical and even mediaeval men and women could just about take in the world in which they lived with a naive glance. It was finite; the infinite world of God with angels and saints began immediately above the vault of heaven. The earth was the centre of the whole cosmos, around which everything else turned. And human beings were above all creatures of the Most High, created by God in his image and exalted above all other creatures, who had to serve them. Human beings were the focus of God's interest. World history was played out between them and their God. The course of this history determined the fate of the whole cosmos.

Biblical people could only articulate their experience of God and their faith in images, terminology and ideas which corresponded to the world-view of the ancient Near East or antiquity. The naive notion of the earth as the centre of the world and of human beings who live at the centre of divine interest as the goal and crown of creation permeates all that the Bible says about God and the world. It provides the co-ordinates of a system within which almost all traditional church teachings about the faith have been introduced and formulated – down to the new Catholic Catechism. And the prayers and hymns of the liturgy and the majority of all sermons automatically instil the geocentric and anthropocentric view of the world into the heads of believers, often linking it indissolubly with faith.

But today we know that the earth on which we human beings live is only a small planet orbiting the sun. And our solar system is only one of the many millions of solar systems which orbit in the spirals of our galaxy, the Milky Way. And there are said to be around two billion galaxies.

Such dimensions are mind-boggling. Even a speck of dust is bigger in relation to the globe than the globe is in relation to the expanding universe. Moreover, I read recently that scientists are now saying that our cosmos is not even the only one. It is embedded in a far greater cosmos, in a mega-cosmos. Like our universe, which has been expanding like a 'cosmic bubble' since the so-called Big Bang and one day will contract again in a reverse movement of time and space, new cosmic bubbles, new universes, are constantly arising from a so-called 'primal foam'. Before the Big Bang was the primal foam.

From this perspective, our unimaginably large universe contracts into a 'local affair'. So physicists are now speaking of a 'multiverse'. The Russian physicist Andrei Dmietrevich Linde comments: 'Previously it was thought that before the Big Bang there was nothing, afterwards everything. Now we need no longer assume that there is a single universe which came into being out of nothing and represents the beginning of all space-time.'

It is not surprising that thinking and informed people are finding it increasingly difficult to put any trust in the usual church language. This geocentric and anthropocentric view reduces and narrows down the whole immeasurable universe with its physical, chemical and biological processes, over unimaginable periods of time, and with the incomprehensibly complex development of life, to human beings. That contradicts everything that we know about the world and human beings today and is untenable.

The world – '. . .created for the church'?

A naive view of the world with the idea of the earth as its
centre decisively shaped the views of God in the church and in
the Bible. The scientist Hoimar von Ditfurth points out that the
mediaeval notion of a God who is enthroned over the earth, and
with his glorified Son exercises rule at the head of heavenly
hosts, archangels, angels and saints, is a sociomorphic projection. Here the social structures of the ancient and mediaeval
feudal order of society are unconsciously projected on to the
image of God.

What was believed to be the hierarchical structure of the
heavenly world was necessarily projected back on to earthly and
human social orders. It confirmed and legitimated the position
of the pope at the head of many cardinals, archbishops, bishops
and prelates and the secular rule of the emperor at the head of
the social pyramid in a feudal order.

Against this background we can understand the vigorous
defensive reactions of the church when towards the end of the
Middle Ages Copernicus dethroned the earth from its central
position. It also explains the condemnation of Galileo.
Giordano Bruno, who was probably the first to recognize how
theologically explosive this changed geocentric picture was, had
to pay for the theological conclusions which he drew from it
with death at the stake. The papal Inquisition also sensed the
threat posed to the church's rule over souls by the new picture
of the world. If what Copernicus claimed was really true, then
in the long run the whole intellectual structure of a well-ordered
cosmic hierarchy centred on God was doomed to collapse, and
with it the rationale for the church's hierarchy.

However, if God's history with the world is centred on God's
action on earthly human beings, the pope and the bishops come
to the centre of world history. Indeed the whole immeasurable
cosmos, which has been expanding from the Big Bang for more
than sixteen billion years, finds the key to its completion in God
in the church and its leaders. 'The world was created for the

sake of the Church. The Church is the goal of all things'
(1/ no.760).

Such statements could only be made by those who saw the
earth and human beings at the centre of the whole universe. But
since this is no longer the accepted view today, they are interpreted as the expression of an arrogance in which error has
become delusion about the centre.

What kind of a view is it that God has produced the
immeasurable universe, billions of light years across, with all
its complicated physical, chemical, biological, psychological,
spiritual and cultural processes, at so many levels, so that this
universe could reach its goal in the Roman church with the pope
at its head?

In Eugen Drewermann's book about Giordano Bruno, Bruno
says to his accusers: 'You are incapable of seeing that God has
not created an infinite universe in order to occupy himself for
the future exclusively with the history of the inhabitants of one
small planet' (3/148).

Come down from heaven?

The doctrine that the Son of God has come down to earth and
become man there stands at the centre of Christian faith.

It could only have been formulated in this way with a picture
of the world which saw the earth and human beings at the
centre of the whole universe. It is bound up in a view of the
world which no longer holds today.

As long as human knowledge of the world did not extend
much further than people could see with the naked eye, and they
thought of their little earth and themselves as the centre of the
whole creation, they had no difficulty in imagining that deities
who lived immediately above the earth could descend and walk
on the earth as human beings: the Acts of the Apostles tells how
the apostle Paul and his companion Barnabas were regarded as

gods in Lystra: 'The gods have come down to us in human form'
(Acts14.11).

The notion that God, the creator of the universe, became
incarnate on earth, a cosmic speck of dust, in a human being, a
chance product of evolution, could only have been formulated
by people whose view of the world was imprisoned in a quite
naive geocentricity and anthropocentricity, and who through no
fault of their own knew nothing of the real position of human
beings in the cosmos.

Of course I know that the phrase 'God's Son came down
from heaven and became man' is only one of the many
inadequate attempts to depict figuratively experiences arising
out of an encounter with the person of Jesus. Like the image
'ascended into heaven', it is an image in mythical language.
Indeed, this mythical formula is a good image which can help
to express and developed what dawned on people after their
encounter with Jesus: his bond with God. But it remains
meaningful only if we are aware that it is a figurative way of
speaking.

However, in current church teaching, from the preaching of
the village pastor to the pope's Christmas address, it is not interpreted as an image but described as a real historical event: God
sent to earth his Son, begotten before all time. There he became
a human being in the womb of a virgin. The pope explicitly
teaches in the Catechism: 'Belief in the true Incarnation is the
distinctive sign of Christian faith' (1/ no.463).

Only if we allow this doctrine to stand as an image arising
out of a naive view of the world can the truth which was
originally intended by it be handed down over the ages. If we
follow the pope in understanding the metaphor of the descent of
a Son of God as the depiction of an actual event, we distort the
original meaningful point of this image so much that it becomes
nonsensical.

From a static to an evolutionary picture of the world

The change from a static to an evolutionary picture of the world which was pioneered a century ago by Darwin is likely to be even more momentous for faith than the collapse of the geocentric picture of the world as a result of the discoveries of modern astronomy since Copernicus.

Darwin's recognition that plants, animals and human beings have developed in long historical processes has now become an axiom in almost all sciences, far beyond the sphere of biology. Everything that exists in the world has a long history of development behind it. This development has many branches, and is often directed by chance. Nothing has always been as it is now. Nothing will remain as it is now. Everything will develop further and change. Nothing is finished. Ours is a world in becoming.

The whole universe developed in a process of physical and chemical evolution over an unimaginably vast period which physicists calculate at between fifteen and twenty billion years. According to the scientists, the universe has come into being. Our planet on which we live, the earth, is the result of the contraction of a floating cloud of gas about four and a half billion years ago. As the history of the earth shows us, the continents, with the deserts and mountains and hills, all formed, rose and sank, shifted, folded and overlapped over long periods. And the constant change goes on.

The development of life on earth was similar. After the cooling of the surface, in a long and complicated prehistory the first life organized itself out of simple chemical bonds; over more than three billion years it then diversified into the countless types of plants and animals.

We human beings also have our roots in this history of development. We are closely related to the animals, particularly to the higher mammals. By chance mutations and selections, the antecedents of present-day human beings developed through amphibians, reptiles and mammals. And it was still a long way from these early hominids, in the transitional stage between animals and human beings, to *homo sapiens* with many unsuccessful experiments on the way, and through numerous intermediate stages like *homo habilis* or *homo erectus*.

There is no reason at all to suppose that this evolutionary process has been completed. The development of human beings is still in process. We do not know where it will lead to. We today are the Neanderthals for those human beings who will live on this globe in fifty thousand years – if anyone is living on it at all then! Present-day human beings are a transitional product with an open future. And there is also no compelling reason to assume that as a biological species we will fare differently from millions of other species before us: they died out.

We carry within us the legacy of hundreds of millions of years of biological prehistory, not only in our physical structure and functions but in our behaviour, thought, feeling, experience and values. We are endowed with the quite contradictory legacy of our biological, psychological and cultural tribal history.

Behavioural research and investigations into the development of intellectual capacity have shown quite clearly how our thought and behaviour are shaped by our ancestry. Even the cultural traditions followed laws similar to those governing biological evolution.

Would the religions be an exception here? Would the Christian religion be an exception from the other religions? Wouldn't religious notions also have developed in a similar way?

Most of those who hold office in the church and most theologians have yet to realize what dynamite there is in the arsenals of an evolutionary interpretation of the world.

Church thought – evolutionary thought

Only in 1950 did Pope Pius, in his encyclical *Humani generis,* 'allow' (!) the 'investigation of the origin of human life from already existing animate matter'. The church's magisterium still does not seem to have taken account of the development of our spiritual and intellectual capacities and our social behaviour from prior forms in our ancestry which experts now take for granted. No more than a brief look at the new Catechism will show this.

The mere recognition, prompted by knowledge of evolution, that everything that is in the world has developed from below upwards, starting with simple beginnings and becoming higher and more complex, leading to the human capacities for thinking and loving, indeed for thinking about God, is quite diametric- ally opposed to the traditional hierarchical thought-structures of the church. Here everything – spirit, truth, life, love and also power – comes from above downwards.

The notion that doctrines contain and preserve 'unalterable eternal truths' and 'norms of behaviour which transcend time' is clearly stuck in an outdated, static picture of the world. If the church became open to the evolutionary view of the world in its thinking, it would have to recognize that both its doctrines and its norms of behaviour have formed over history. They have no finality and must constantly change. Like all that lives!

I now understand why the church is instinctively defensive about changes in world-views. Because the whole structure of its faith is grounded in the world-view of antiquity, any change in the world-view must shake the foundations of that structure. It is no coincidence that the church has still failed in its theology to take in the discoveries of Copernicus, Bruno, Galileo, Darwin and Freud. All too many doctrines and directives would have had to be corrected. And that too would have put everything into the melting pot, including the infallibility of the magis- terium.

No wonder that so many church dignitaries are more afraid

of the modern scientific view of the world than the devil is of holy water!

Translation for today?

Of course our view of the world, which follows from countless individual insights in a great variety of sciences, is incomplete. A multitude of details need constantly to be developed, checked, corrected and supplemented. Moreover, one day it too will certainly become outdated and be dropped. However, there is no way back to the picture of the world to which the church clings.

Until the beginning of modern times the Christian faith was convincing largely because it corresponded to existing views of the world. Faith and knowledge were in agreement. Since the Enlightenment and the rise of modern science, this harmony has increasingly been strained, and there will be yet further drifting apart, as with the continents. What people know and what the church asks them to believe will move further and further apart.

If the church compels people to believe in notions based on an outdated view of the world, it will make faith seem out of date, and drive more and more people away.

It seems to me to be the great task of theology, present and future, to assimilate the great changes in the present-day view of the world and human nature, in order to open up the abiding truth of Christian faith once again to men and women of today and tomorrow.

Understood less and less

Here are some remarks by Hoimar von Ditfurth, who made me think hard years ago.

'If it is to be not only correct but comprehensible, theology will have to take account of the findings and the progress of the scientific explanation of the world. At all events, neither the theologian nor the lay believer can go on escaping the influence of evolutionary thought. The only way of doing this would be to isolate themselves, in an act of intellectual violence, from the world-view of their contemporaries. Those who do that should not complain if they find themselves cut off. Those who quarantine their thought and language from the central intellectual currents of our time may be able to secure an audience on the basis of an inherited authority, but they will become increasingly incomprehensible.

For a long time there has been no reason to fear contagion from the picture of an evolving world which scientists have developed in recent decades. On the contrary, this picture seems to me to offers linguistic images and theoretical models which can be use to formulate central theological statements in a more open and therefore more convincing way than was possible within the static world-view in which theology is still stuck' (20/256).

Restoring the unity

It is assumed that religious and scientific questions have to be carefully distinguished. I cannot agree. I cannot hold one thing to be true if I think in a religious way and quite the opposite to be true if I think in a scientific way. That is schizophrenia, and I cannot honestly go along with it. Certainly I can accept different answers, but not contradictions. Many of my own difficulties with traditional views of faith in the church lie precisely at this point, where the traditional understanding of faith in the church and the present-day world-view meet.

The changed view of the world and human life which I discovered as I grappled with the views of modern science drove me towards an understanding of faith which was not anachronistic and would make it possible for me to go on believing. But at the same time the church's interpretation of its faith, which under Pope John Paul II was again brought out and imposed on the faithful, forced me back into the past. The gulf between the two has grown for me and I am increasingly troubled by doubts. I cannot live – or believe – with this schizophrenia.

These notes are simply my own attempt to restore unity between my faith and the present-day view of the world. They are quite personal. But I hope that they may help others.

3

What is religion good for?

Religion?

Religion has played a relatively major role in my life. Now, in retrospect, I find myself asking why it had become so important for me. What is religion? What are religions good for? What brings them into being? What role do they play in the lives of individuals and humankind?

We can note how religions have formed in all cultures and are an influence at all levels of human existence. According to the ethnologists there is no people on this earth among which manifestations of religious behaviour cannot be noted. It is almost impossible to describe the many ways in which religion manifests itself in human existence.

Especially in countries in which life has been governed by religion almost without a break and which so far have hardly been exposed to any critical questioning, for example in the Islamic world, and also in India and Nepal, I have experienced what deep roots religion has in the human soul and how fundamental is the human need for religion. Almost everywhere I went in those countries, and almost everything I saw, showed religion as a force in all human activity.

Time and again, I could not avoid noting how fundamentally similar human forms of religious behaviour are, despite all the differences in the religions and despite the difference in forms of religious expression as a result of cultural conditioning.

Religious behaviour is certainly subject to cultural variations, but its patterns of behaviour seem to have a fundamentally genetic structure. Moreover they are communicated genetically.

In varied forms

Religion ranges from the mythical interpretations of life among primitive peoples, the wisdom teachings of Buddha and Koheleth/Ecclesiastes, through the parables of the Gospels, the surahs of the Qur'an, the *Summa* of Thomas Aquinas and the revivalist preaching of American sects to papal encyclicals. It manifests itself in the magic of the medicine man and the consecrations performed by the pope. It extends from feathers in the hair to mitres on the heads of bishops. It extends from bans and taboos to excommunication by the church, from intolerant fanaticism which burns those of other faiths at the stake, to unselfish, loving sacrifice in the service of the poor, the weak and the sick.

Human ideas of God range from magical nature deities through the capricious gods of Olympus to the notion of a single personal God in the biblical religions; from ideas of cruel divine despots who had to be offered bloody animal and human sacrifices in order to pacify them, to the belief in a Son of God who sacrificed himself on the cross in order to reconcile humankind with God. The span of religion extends from the Pharaonic sons of god in Egypt through Heracles the divine son, swinging his cudgel, and the Roman emperor who bore the title son of god, to the humbly obedient divine sonship of Jesus of Nazareth; from the archaic fertility goddesses through the Egyptian Isis and the sensuous goddesses of antiquity, to Mary the chaste virgin mother of God.

Religion expresses itself in the rhythmic stamping of cultic dances among African peoples, in the Gregorian chant of monks, in the choral works of Bach and the inwardness of Mozart's *'Ave verum'*, in the bewitching cave paintings of Altamira, in the Byzantine frescoes, in Raphael's madonnas and in the hovering angels of Marc Chagall.

Religion unites the healing medicine men in the bush and the healing god Asclepius of Epidaurus with Jesus' healings of the sick, the pilgrimage places of the Middle Ages and the healing brought by the madonnas of Kevelaer and Lourdes. Religion is localized in sacred springs and stones, in the temples by the Nile and the pagodas by the Ganges, in the mediaeval cathedrals and also in the imitation of the dome of St Peter's in the African steppe. Religion unites the dancing dervish with the officiating prelate.

The vast variety of religious phenomena with their branches and similarities demonstrates that religions, too, undergo processes of development and cultural differentiation. Just as we speak of a history of biological and cultural evolution, so too we could speak of a history of religious evolution.

A *matter of geography*

My daughter lives right in the north of Germany near the Danish border. I visited her and also got to know the people who had become important in her life. In the evening we sat together in the garden. My daughter and I were the only Catholics; all the rest were Protestants. Somehow the conversation got round to the confessional question. Despite all the tolerance and courteous amiability of my conversation partners, which was genuine, I sensed from their remarks that beyond question they felt that they were practising a form of Christian faith which was superior to Catholicism. – When I am in Bavaria or Austria or even in Spain, I have the same experience, but the other way round.

How does it come about that people acquire and promote a particular religious conviction? Although my way to belief was very much an intellectual one, and I arrived at faith through intensive intellectual arguments, I ask myself whether I would have become a Catholic had I been born, say, the son of Protestant parents in Schleswig-Holstein and grown up in the strongly Protestant milieu there, instead of having been born in the Catholic milieu of the Rhineland. Would my intellectual arguments still have led me to the Catholic Church? I doubt it.

And what if I had been born in Cairo, the son of the bazaar stallholder Ali ben Muhammad? Would I then have become a convinced Islamic teacher of the Qur'an? What if Karol Wojtyla had grown up only a few hundred miles further East? Would he now be the patriarch of an Orthodox church?

Are religious convictions a matter of geography?

Caught up in a process of socialization

This short concrete enquiry has already made it clear to me how little the formation of religious convictions has to do with the laborious intellectual process of seeking and knowing 'truth'. What the religions call 'truth' is not 'known' in them by cognitive efforts, but quite simply adopted in a process of socialization.

Religious convictions are acquired in a process of growing into the ways of thought, the patterns of behaviour and the spiritual traditions of a milieu. There is usually little reflection on this process. Psychologists speak of an internalization of pre-existing socially communicated values. As a rule, these socially communicated basic convictions are assimilated by reflection; only subsequently, if at all, are they given a rational foundation.

Behavioural science has developed the concept of moulding. Konrad Lorenz originally used this concept to describe the adoption of vitally necessary modes of behaviour, using the social bonding of new-born grey geese to their mother as an example. Moulding is a pre-cognitive learning process. Among human beings, moulding of a social, cultural or religious nature might have developed out of what were initially biological processes. Konrad Lorenz has often referred to the similarity between biological and cultural moulding. Such moulding also occurs among young people when they adopt modes of thinking, evaluation and behaviour from their social environment. The adoption and appropriation of religious convictions also seems to me to be largely the result of such moulding.

If the amiable monk who guided me through his monastery in Baghdapur in Nepal was a convinced Buddhist, it was probably because he had been moulded by this religion from his childhood on. If the Egyptian teacher who showed me the temple buildings of Luxor was a convinced Muslim, this was probably because his thought had been moulded by the religion of his environment. And why did Cardinal Ratzinger become a convinced Catholic Christian?

Moulding is usually an irreversible process. It largely resists rational investigation. As a rule, those who have been moulded by a particular culture or religious conviction remain bound to this conviction all their lives.

What impels people into religion?

What really impels people into religion? What makes them open and ready to adopt religious teaching, rules of behaviour and rituals? What psychological disposition and motivation to religious behaviour is common to Hindus, Muslims, Buddhists, Jews and Christians and all the different adherents of other religious groups?

It would certainly be wrong to want to derive religious practice from a single cause in human beings. The roots of human religion are grounded in many very different strata of human life.

One of its roots may already lie in an elementary biological and social form of safeguarding existence. Anxious about their daily food, primitive people sought the support of deities to give them good luck in hunting and fertility. Another root grows from the deeper spiritual need for security and comfort. Religions provide rules and guidelines for life. Religions help people to find a place for themselves in the midst of an impenetrable existence.

The longing for an ultimate authority which can give support and certainty to life, and the quest of the human spirit for reliable truth which sheds light on the darkness of the way, also lead people to religion. Religion grows from the longing for a meaning in life which resists all the contradictions that are experienced. The longing of the human heart for a Thou who can be trusted to the end, a personal encounter which offers the possibility of dialogue, also opens people to religion.

Born of a human anxiety about existence?

Many – but not all – of the different sources of human religion seem to derive from a common ground: anxiety. Do religions feed on human anxiety about existence in its many forms, open and disguised?

Anxiety helps to protect life. It is an aid to survival. It already begins in the anxiety of animals about enemies who may devour them. It is also a force in the life of human beings who from primeval times have experienced uncertainty, exposure and manifold threats to their existence in this world. Anxiety grows out of the experience of the inadequacy of human power to banish disaster from life.

Unknown threats deepen anxiety. Religions promise to bring liberation from anxiety. And they do so. Belief in a deity whom one knows and can influence through cultic rituals, through sacrifice, through prayers and submission, diminishes anxiety about the many unknown threats.

The human desire to secure the support of a powerful deity is understandable. The unconscious memory of a protective security which one received in childhood from a strong father or a caring mother is transferred to the deity. This deity can then take on the features of the loving father, as in the New Testament, or the face of a mother deity graciously inclining herself, under whose protective cloak human distress seeks perpetual help, as in the cult of Mary.

To *ward off disaster?*

Where people see a deity at work behind all events, misfortune and disaster, sickness and death are interpreted as the punitive action of this deity. Then religion becomes an attempt to influence fate; an attempt is made to reconcile active deities through sacrifice, cultic rituals, prayers and submission, and to secure their favour. Here the Christian religion is no exception, particularly in its Catholic form.

Almost everything that religions offer people in their myths and images, rituals and cults, words and teachings, can be understood against the background of anxiety. An analysis of the treasury of prayer handed down in the tradition of the Bible and the church, whether in the church's liturgy or popular piety, will show that it is clearly dominated by prayers for help in distress, for the aversion of some evil, for rescue from destruction.

Probably the deepest root of human readiness to rely on religion may lie in anxiety about death. Is death really to be the end of everything, everything for which one has lived and worked, all one's loves and hopes? Is it a final end? How gladly then people cling to the comforting message that a living God waits beyond the threshold of death, transforms everything into a new, whole life and grants eternity!

Is religion born of anxiety? Anxiety about the nothingness on the periphery of our life? Anxiety about the loss of ground under our feet? Anxiety at the uncertainty of what is coming? Without death would there be no religion?

Produced *by evolution?*

All innate psychological dispositions have their origin in the history of the development of the human psyche. They have formed at some time and in some place, in particular historical conditions, from the free evolutionary interplay of mutations and selections; they have proved advantageous for the survival

of the individual and the species and found a way into hereditary genetic information.

On the basis of all that we know today about the connections
between biological and cultural evolution, it seems to me not
completely erroneous to suppose that human religious
behaviour, too, could have its roots in biological and cultural
evolution. Religion is woven into a network of many processes
conditioned by human development.

I am inclined to see religion, too, as a late result of the
evolutionary unfolding of life. Like 'cultural evolution', the
formation of the religious dimension, too, could be a stage of
development in the further unfolding and higher development
of life from the biological sphere to the human psychological,
social and intellectual sphere.

In that case, like all 'inventions' of evolution, religion too
would serve to preserve and develop life.

To reinforce social cohesion?

Behavioural research speaks of 'bonding measures' in evolution.
In the animal world, for example, these bond individual fishes
into a shoal or birds into a flock, zebras and oxen into herds and
wolves into packs: they consist in the same pattern of colour, the
same smell, the same ritual behaviour, the same acoustic signals,
etc. These serve to reinforce social cohesion and thus to ensure
survival.

Such 'bonding measures' have also been preserved in human
development and act in a modified form: a shared culture, a
shared language, shared forms of behaviour, shared festivals
and rites bring about and reinforce the cohesion of social
groups. They bind individuals together in families, in clans, in
peoples. Flags, costume and songs also fulfil this purpose.

It occurs to me that religion, too, the common worship of a
God, is one of these 'bonding measures' which human tribal
history has produced as an aid to the survival of the human

species. Religion, together with the development of human consciousness, might have emerged in an evolutionary process from prior forms which lead animals, too, to form and maintain orderly groups. At a higher level of evolution, religion would have had a similar function in bonding and direction to those bonding features which can also be found at lower pre-conscious levels of life.

So is religion a 'bonding measure' produced by biological and cultural evolution, which makes it possible for individuals to live together in a larger social group and thus provides the human species with a strategy for survival?

Biblical religion too?

The shared god binds. In the history of religion we can see how the deities held social alliances together. In the early period it was predominantly the small social groups – the family, the clan or the tribe – which bonded into units that aided their survival by the common worship of a god.

Initially the biblical God, too, was the family god of the clan of Abraham which immigrated from Chaldaea, the 'God of Abraham, Isaac and Jacob'. Later Moses combined this 'God of the fathers' with Yahweh, the God of Sinai, to become the God of a people. Worship of this God and obedience to his laws bonded the tribes of Israel into a greater social unity, a people.

As the Bible tells us again and again, the biological survival of Israel indeed depended on loyalty to this God, precisely as Moses and the prophets had kept proclaiming. Only loyalty to the covenant, only unconditional allegiance to this God, held the families, clans and tribes together so that they became the 'people of God', and thus increased Israel's chances of survival in the midst of a world of enemies.

Basically, what took place there was no more and no less than what has taken place in the history of all other peoples on this globe: a large social group fights with other large groups competing for a biological advantage, for opportunities, land and sources of food and for the largest possible number of descendants. And that cannot be done without the notion of a God who 'wants' such a thing. The people's enemies are also the enemies of their God. And the enemies of God must be annihilated. 'God is with us.' That is how it has been down to the present day. All over the world.

The interpretation in the Bible, that God has chosen the people Israel, made a covenant with it, so that it becomes great and strong in a land 'flowing with milk and honey', is a time-conditioned interpretation of Israel's history from the perspective of its own interests.

Religion and war

When I see the biological and social function of religion in connection with the evolution of life, I can also understand better why religions have constantly been entangled in disputes and wars with one another. Even today religions underlie many wars and conflicts: there are the Catholic Croats, the Muslim Bosnians and the Orthodox Serbs in the Balkans; the Shi'ites and Sunnis in the Muslim East; Catholics and Protestants in Ireland; Muslims and Hindus in India.

The issue here is not, as I once quite naively assumed, the establishment of a belief or even of 'truth'. What is happening here is not about truth or even about God at all. It is a competition to establish the vital interests of one group over against another. Religion is one of the values which ultimately all serve to safeguard the biological existence of a people: domination, possession of land, sources of raw material, economic power, etc.

And here the religions form the ideological superstructure. 'We are fighting for God's cause.' 'God is with us.' 'Allah will immediately receive the slain heroes into his paradise.' There have been such slogans at all times, in all peoples and in all religions. Hitherto I always thought that wars of religion were among the greatest errors and mistakes of religions; that at best they were due to human ignorance and blindness, but that at all events they were contrary to the essence of religion. Now, when I see the religions in the context of biological evolution as an instrument for safeguarding the biological survival of a people, I have to think again: religions usually serve to sacralize and legitimize wars. The church and the military have always got on well, and so have bishops and generals. At all times priests have blessed departing armies and their weapons.

Hans Küng is probably right when he says that there can be no peace between the nations as long as there is no peace between the religions.

Powers of order?

Now it is also becoming clear to me why religions and state power have been so closely connected since primal times and work together admirably despite all conflicts.

Both powers have always been a unity. Tribal rulers also performed magical functions in the cult. The Pharaohs of Egypt were sons and incarnations of the deity. The Roman Caesars bore the title of a god. The political rule of the Pontifex Maximus has influenced the present-day papacy. The mediaeval theory of the two swords divided the spiritual and the secular powers, and at the same time bound them into a unity. Imperial rule needed consecration by the pope. Bishops ruled as feudal lords. The priestly rule in the old temples is repeated in the regime of the mullahs in Teheran. Supreme heads of state have also stood at the head of the religious hierarchy, from the Pharaohs to the Queen of England. Don Camillo and Peppone are united, even if they argue.

The historical and personal interlocking of the two powers reflects a relationship between them which in fact exists. The state can stabilize its political authority if it can claim to have been appointed and willed by God. The religions are glad to perform this service. The Christian religion, too, teaches that 'all authority comes from God' (Rom.13.17). The religions provide a basis for the rule of the powerful: they consecrate it, sacralize it, and celebrate it. And they are recompensed for their service with many privileges.

Religion and the power of the state are simply two sides of the same coin. I must think again.

In the service of fertility?

Now I can also understand why the religions almost in unison urge their adherents to have as many offspring as possible: it is the most important interest of biological evolution to develop life in the greatest possible variety and numbers. Evolution has little interest in the fortunes of individuals and their fate. Regardless of whether they are hungry, wretched, suffer or die, the main thing is for them to procreate.

When, despite all the justified warnings against the catastrophic consequences of overpopulation and in awareness of the wretchedness of the Third World, unswervingly and obdurately, the pope still promotes the joys of giving birth and brands birth control an act against God's will, his voice is quite simply that of biological evolution, not the voice of God who – according to Jesus – wants human well-being. The papacy is fulfilling the very function which evolution assigned to religion at its 'invention'.

I think that the prophets of Israel in their fight against the Canaanite fertility deities had already gone further when they set obedience to the 'wholly other God' over against the cult of Baal. The God of Israel was not a fertility god. No God speaks from the voice of the pope unless it is the voice of a fertility god who is simply a personified projection of the biological control of human behaviour.

The god to whom the pope appeals in his calls for fertility is not the God of Jesus.

Religions too arise and pass away

The observation that religions and cultures are subject to similar laws, as instanced in the biological development of life, reinforces my supposition that the religions are part of the biological and cultural evolution of humankind.

In analogy to biological species and individuals, religions usually come into being out of the union and fusion of earlier religions or as branches of them. They were all 'born' at one time, like biological individuals and species, like historical peoples and cultures. Their beginnings are usually pure and near to God. In their youth they flourish and have a springlike radiance. They grow and gain power, magnitude and importance. But at the peak of their development they already become rigid and formal. The spirit-inspired message of their founders, which once won people's hearts, slowly hardens into an objectified doctrine, watched over by learned theologians. The power of the spirit is institutionalized as the rule of priests. Attempts at reform lead to splits. A battle over what is pure doctrine flares up between the rival groups. The institution becomes fossilized. The gulf between the claims of religion and human life becomes greater and greater. Religion loses significance for an increasing number of people.

The Christian religion may be in this phase today. At least in its present-day church form, one day it will no longer exist, just as the religions of Egypt, Mesopotamia, Greece and Rome are no longer there today. The individual religions pass away, like everything else in the world. They lose their force, they become old and tired, they die and pass on, changing into new religions. New deities will cast the old ones from their thrones.

Christianity, too, is a historical religion which had a beginning and will also have an end. Today we are already experiencing an autumnal form of this religion. How long may it still last? Who knows? The life-span of religions is reckoned in millennia.

However, that does not apply to the Catholic Church. As the papal Catechism teaches, it is 'indestructible' (1/ no.869).

4

God is different

What is meant by God?

To be quite honest, I have to concede that even now I still do not know what is really meant by the word 'God'. Although I have been thinking about God almost all my life, I have not succeeded in being clear what I mean when I say 'God'. And if I already think that I know what the word 'God' means, then the very next day it becomes questionable to me again. Certainly I can repeat many formulae from the language of the religions and even explain some of them; but that does not meant that I know who or what God is. Indeed I am not even sure whether God really exists.

I always admire people who talk about God with such certainty and conviction, as if they knew precisely what God wants or does not want. But they do not speak about God well. The more loudly a church preacher goes on about God, the less he or she has understood God.

'Thank God, there is no such thing as what sixty to eighty per cent of our contemporaries imagine by God,' said Karl Rahner. Perhaps one could go even further: 'Thank God, there is no such thing as what all human beings have so far understood by God.' For what we call 'God' fundamentally transcends the knowledge and understanding of *all* human beings, even that of great theologians and thinkers, and certainly also that of the pope and the bishops.

A reflection of the soul against an infinite horizon?

Traditional church thought and talk about God is governed by the notion of an eternal, unchangeable, perfect God who was always there in his perfection before all time and as an infinite God brought forth a finite world.

However, with all due respect to this exalted notion of God, I must nevertheless ask whether it, too, has not grown up in history. Isn't it, too, subject to the limitations of human thought and language? This classical notion interprets the relationship between God and the world deductively, i.e. from above downwards. It is rooted in the static view of the world characteristic of antiquity.

Anyone who is familiar with the evolutionary view of the world and has adopted its perspective cannot avoid rethinking some traditional human ideas and seeking a new understanding. That is also the case with the question of God. So in the question of God, I also look for an inductive approach from below, from human existence. How has the idea of a God come into being in the course of human development?

It has struck me that everything that the religions say about God, about God's power, about how God is beyond our control and powers of description, and about how the destinies of human beings are dependent on his favour, are at the same time also statements which could be made quite generally about life and the way in which human destiny is woven into the structures of this life, even without God. That makes me wonder whether all the statements of the religions about God and the divine could not fundamentally be simply reflections of human experiences of life itself.

In that case every question about God would be quite simply a question about life, about its foundations, its meaning, its character and its rules. In that case all the answers which the religions offer people are simply an assimilation and interpretation of human experiences which have been projected on to a divine power or person.

In that case, what we call God would itself be a projection, a reflection of the human soul on the horizon of infinity.

God – 'innate'?

Already in the early period of humankind, when human beings began to stand upright and for the first time it dawned on their consciousness that the world was something other than themselves, an inkling of divine powers may also have awoken in them. Experiences of the impenetrable interconnections in life, on which flourishing and decay, salvation and disaster were dependent, could not yet be assimilated rationally and interpreted. They became concentrated and objectified in the notion of active invisible powers, active deities. These 'deities' were the primeval ancestors of all the later gods: personified powers of destiny. The early deities were probably first approached in magical rituals through which human beings sought to influence their fate and banish threats.

When the dawning human consciousness in primeval times gropingly penetrated the darkness of life with its questions; when primeval hands for the first time scratched mysterious signs on stone to influence an unknown power which determined fate, from when human language for the first time stammered a word for 'God', 'God' was taken into human consciousness and as an image left an indelible mark on the soul.

We have all inherited God from our ancestors. God is 'innate' in us. God keeps breaking through in people. God cannot be silenced. No atheistic programme of education nor any millionfold misuse of God's name has been able to suppress God from the consciousness of humankind.

Since then God has been in every human being who is born: as an image, a claim, a power, a riddle, a question, a reality. And everyone has to see how he or she deals with this heritage.

Images of God: dependent on culture

The notions of divine powers keep changing in human history. They share all the stages of the development of the human soul and the human spirit. Images from the changing spheres of human experience, and from our geographical and cultural environment, make their mark on our image of deity.

How a particular idea of God is filled with content and imagery depends on the particular historical, social or cultural environment. It is not handed on genetically but culturally.

Thus God's countenance is not the same for an Indian in the Amazon basin and for someone living in the deserts of the East; the cultural factors which govern the image of God for a Tibetan in the Himalayas are not those which govern the image of God for believers in Mediterranean cultures.

'God' does not descend from heaven complete, to take a place in human consciousness. God becomes! In humankind and in every individual.

Another name for fate?

How did human beings come to believe in the existence of a God? What are the anthropological roots of belief in God in human experience?

Human beings experience pieces of good fortune in their lives: deliverance from extreme distress, preservation from death, an unmerited act of benevolence. Who changed their fortunes? Who rescued them? Who preserved them? Who showed them kindness? Who else but a God: a God who is 'with us', a God who is to be thanked?

Such experiences also underlie the biblical belief in God.

Disaster broke in unexpectedly: an earthquake which destroyed everything; a storm which wrought wholesale devastation; a sickness which thwarted all plans; a famine or a war which threatened life. Who made the walls of the house collapse? Who made the fields wither? Who gave power to the enemy? Who else but a God, a God who was insulted, a God who had to be reconciled?

Such experiences and interpretations also stand at the beginning of the biblical faith.

From the very beginning, human beings have kept experiencing how the fortunes of life, its wholeness and its disasters, are inextricably interwoven into a network of compelling facts and chance events which cannot be planned. They have experienced how it is dependent on 'powers and authorities' over which they have no control. Who imposed the fate? Who decreed it? Who planned the unplanned? Who else but a God: an incalculable God who has to be influenced by rites, sacrifices and prayers?

Is the word 'God' perhaps just another name for an inscrutable fate which is beyond our control?

The birth of the gods

The suspicion keeps forcing itself upon me that in the history of religion, inexplicable forces beyond human control which determined the fate of a people or an individual have been interpreted as the action of supernatural personal powers. These were personalized, projected into a supernatural sphere and thus divinized.

In this way the gods were born. The dependence of the survival of the individual and society on a wealth of children found its personalized and divinized projection in the seductive Venus, in the many-breasted Artemis and the countless mother deities. The dependence of Egypt on the inundation of the Nile turned the Nile itself into a god. Where rain ensured a people its food, altars were erected to the deities who gave rain. The life-threatening unpredictability of the sea was personalized and divinized in the capricious sea god Poseidon, just as the uncertainty of fortunes in war and hunting was personalized and divinized in the numerous gods of war and the hunt.

Is God another name for life itself?

What about the biblical God?

As someone whose belief in God stands in the biblical tradition, I would gladly exclude the God of Israel, who was also the God of Jesus, from this list and claim a special status for him. That is the course usually adopted by church teaching, in which I too was involved. But is it honest?

Doesn't the biblical God, too – like the deities of primeval times and the great gods of Egypt, Babylon, India, Greece or Rome – owe his existence to a historical human interpretation of existence in which the forces of nature and events that determined people's fates were interpreted as the personal action of a divine person? I cannot see any compelling reason for excluding the biblical God, and thus also the Christian God, from this list, however much I would like to. Still, the biblical belief in God remains the norm for my own belief.

In this monotheistic notion of God, the many forms of the forces which determine life are concentrated in a single person. Certainly the God of Israel was not a divinized power of nature. Israel's God was Lord of the forces of nature, not part of them. Israel's faith de-divinized nature, and this gave rise to an idea of God which was completely new in the history of religion: a personal God active in history. But the biblical notion of God, too, is a concentration of the powers that shape destiny, which Israel experienced in history.

Did the biblical God emerge from Israel's interpretation of its existence?

I am now fairly certain that in reality much did not take place as teachers of religion and preachers tell us. It was the other way round.

God did not choose the fleeing Hebrews as 'his people'. Rather, Moses chose 'Yahweh', a god from the Sinai, as God of his wandering people. The god Yahweh was not tied to a local sanctuary but was a deity who travelled around with nomadic groups of shepherds. So he was pre-eminently suited to accompanying the wandering Hebrews and binding them together as a people.

God did not give the 'law' to the people on Sinai. Rather, in the period of the wandering in the wilderness and even later, after the Israelite settlement in Palestine, rules of behaviour and laws were framed. They had many levels and some of them were rooted in the different traditions of other peoples. Although they were the work of human beings, they were attributed to the God of Moses as Israel's lawgiver. They reflect not only a wise assimilation of social experiences but also the limited horizon, the lack of humanity and the prejudices of an ancient Near Eastern society with a patriarchal structure. The Ten Commandments and the numerous laws were to some extent 'put in the mouth' of the God of Moses and sealed with his authority.

God did not 'create human beings in his own image'. On the contrary: human beings created God in their image. The image of the biblical God, too, is characterized by the thought and the ideas, the anxieties, expectations and hopes of the people of Israel. This God is a caring God who is always there, the God Israel needed in danger, a patriarchal God with the features of the social structure of nomadic groups.

The 'people' is not the 'son of God' or 'children of God' – as we read in the Old Testament. Here too it is the other way round: this God is a 'son of Israel', a 'child' of this people, born of its time-conditioned notions, modes of thought and needs. This God is a creation of Israel and bears its features. He is a projection from the psyche of Israel. The image of God in the Bible also came into being in history and grew up with Israel's consciousness. The image of God is an image of the people who painted it: a copy of themselves, a copy of their image of life, a copy of their image of the world.

We say something very like this about the ideas of God in

other religions, almost as a matter of course. But in the case of our biblical Christian God we reject the suspicion. Are we right?

A son of the desert

I went to the 'Holy Land' with my wife for two weeks to get to know the places of the Bible. We broke our flight home for a few days in Athens. From the window of our hotel room we could see the Acropolis. My wife wanted to rest from the rigours of the journey, but I immediately felt the urge to go up to the citadel of the old Greek gods.

Already while I was climbing the steps to the Propylaion and saw the mighty pillars against a deep blue sky, an inexplicable sense of festivity, an inner relaxation, came over me. It was as if suddenly a pressure, a weight, had dropped from me. Everything became brighter, lighter, freer and more friendly. The cheerful gods of Greece had welcomed me. They had rid me of the heaviness of the land of the Bible.

There for the first time I became aware that I had never felt a sense of cheerfulness and levity in the holy places of the land of the Bible. The God of the Bible is not a cheerful God. He cannot laugh joyfully. He does not enjoy wine. He is a son of the desert. He is like many people who still live in Palestine and the Near East: a projection of the psyche of those who drew his picture.

The only God

Is it a coincidence that the monotheistic notion of God developed in areas with monoform desert landscapes? In religious education we have become used to seeing the origin of belief in a single God in the biblical tradition as a decisive breakthrough in the revelation of the true God, and to devaluing the 'primitive' polytheism of pagan religions by contrast. I've taken this line. But is it really justified?

Historically, it is possible that biblical monotheism had its first beginnings in the religion of ancient Egypt. For a short period (c.1375-1350 BC) the Pharaoh Amenophis IV, better known under the name of Akenaten, established the cult of a single god in Amarna against the resistance of the priesthood: the cult of the sun god Aten. The many deities returned to the temples under his successor Tutenkhamen. To the delight of the priests!

At this time the ancestors of the people of Israel, the Hebrews, were living as slaves in Egypt. We cannot exclude the possibility that when they later escaped from Egypt under the leadership of Moses, they took the notion of the one God with them on their wanderings through the desert and shaped it into belief in Yahweh, the only God, who 'tolerates no other gods beside himself'. The biblical Psalm 104 has an almost literal counterpart in an Egyptian hymn to the sun god Aten (8/ 106f.).

The return of the gods

The notion of the one God who is responsible for everything, which established itself in the biblical tradition in centuries of struggle, often asked too much of Israel's faith. Time and again people kept eyeing the many other gods, and were famously chastized for this by the prophet Elijah. However, the monotheistic notion of God also brought problems, since God was now not just the source of all the good that happened to his people. Now he also had to become responsible for all the evil and suffering in the world and had to listen to the complaints of Job.

In order to relieve the only God of responsibility for evil, he was later saddled with an evil counterpart, the devil, upon whom all evil was now foisted. I can understand why Cardinal Ratzinger still defends belief in the devil. Any God who is thought of in monotheistic terms virtually calls for the invention of a devil. This is the only way in which his hands can be kept clean.

With the many saints who have entered the Christian heaven, exalted by the church to 'the honour of altars', and there have been entrusted with the most varied responsibilities, the old polytheistic gods have re-entered heaven secretly and unrecognized. Even now they maintain a low profile. The women have their necklines rather higher and the men have also adapted themselves to the spiritual milieu: they are somewhat more serious and less sensuous. Be this as it may, in the garb of the Christian saints the old gods have already successfully conspired to undermine the absolutist monotheism.

Granted, their altars no longer stand in temples, but they are there in the niches and chapels of Catholic churches. There the same prayers rise to them as once rose in Epidaurus, Ephesus or Luxor. And when one speaks the right prayers in the right sequence, offers them a sacrifice or at least lights a candle, one can secure their favour, so that from heaven they give help to cure gout, to find a lost bunch of keys or to pass an examination.

What is the difference from the old gods? Here Judaism and Islam are more consistent in their monotheism. But they also draw it daily fresh from the wilderness.

To explain the inexplicable?

Do I need God to understand why the sun shines, why it rains or snows, why lightning flashes from heaven or thunder rumbles? To be honest, no! I can do that better with meteorology.

Do I need God to understand why an avalanche swallows up a village, why an earthquake destroys what it took generations to create, why droughts bring starvation to human beings and animals and the raging rivers in flood bury life beneath them? No – I understand that better with physics and geology.

Do I need God to understand why flowers bloom and trees bear fruit, why lovers come together and why a child is born? No – biology explains that to me better.

Do I need God to understand why cancer eats through the intestines and viruses nest in the cells of the body, why all beauty withers, why a beloved person suffers pain, and why all life, including my own, yields to death? No! Biology and medicine help me to understand that better, although even they cannot answer the ultimate questions.

Do I need God to understand why people are good to one another, love, support and forgive one another? Do I need God or his mythical counterpart, the devil, to explain why human beings succumb to evil, why they murder, rob, lie, hate and cannot live together in peace? – No, here research into behaviour and evolution, psychology and sociology, proves more illuminating for me.

Whenever the name 'God' is mentioned all too quickly in the answers to such questions, I have the suspicion that people have made things too easy for themselves. Instead of investigating causes at many levels and in all their complexity, making an effort to analyse them carefully, they take the easy way out and simply say 'God'. They misuse the name of God, out of intellectual laziness.

I will never be tempted to adopt this way to God. If God is merely a name to help us to understand the incomprehensible, to explain the inexplicable, to control the uncontrollable, then using it is a sin against the second commandment: 'You shall not take the name of God in vain.'

No cover-ups with God

In the terminology of the religions the name of God is all too often misused in order to smooth over the contradictions in life. The name of God serves to paper over the rifts in the structure of the world and to conceal its abysses. It is certainly meant to veil the uncertainty and banish the anxiety.

It is more honest to address the inconsistencies of life, to endure its contradictions and uncertainties, without overhastily allowing oneself to be reassured and comforted with a reference to God. That doesn't do justice to God.

God is not an 'opium of the people'.

Does God send rain?

The notion that a powerful deity is up there who, besieged with people's cries, graciously inclines himself, intervenes in earthly events and sends saving help, is part of the core of all religions. In tribulation Israel cried out to its God Yahweh. All the writings of the Old Testament are permeated with praise of God's saving intervention in history. In accordance with Jesus' encouragement to 'pray in trust to the Father at all times', the church too encourages its faithful to address their petitions to heaven. There not only does God hear them, but they also find a friendly hearing with Mary the mother of God and numerous saints. I have to confess that I too have prayed for God's help in difficult times. It is human to pray. Nevertheless I must answer the question with complete honesty:

Is what we call God an authority, a power, a person who is somewhere above us and who from there intervenes in our fate when we ask him to? Is that really the case?

A God who sends rain when hungry and thirsty people go through the barren fields in procession and call upon him; a God who commands the raging storm and stills the waves of the sea when seafarers cry out to him? – No, I don't believe that any more.

A God who heals the cancer growing in a young woman's breast? A God who restores sight to the blind and recalls the dying to life? A God who restores an adulterous husband to an ageing wife? A God who gives all human beings their daily bread? A God who rewards the good, punishes evil and restores justice? A God who granted the Christian fleet victory over the Turks at Lepanto? A God who gives special illumination and authority to the Catholic popes and bishops?

No I do not see either God or prayer like this. Nor does any Mother of God intervene from heaven when the tears of countless faithful stream down, whether they live in Lourdes or Fatima, Altötting or Kevelaer. – No, I don't believe that.

Such notions of God are certainly human, but they are humanly very naive, anthropomorphic. A God who is spoken of like this is born in the hearts of countless sufferers. He is the projection of their hopes, their anxieties, their longing and their distress.

The religions live by this God who is besieged daily by millions of prayers, to whom millions of candles are lit every day. He provides them with most of their credentials and an even great part of their income. Since primeval times the priests have owed their power to the naive human expectation that they could change fate by influencing the will of a deity by magical rituals and sacrifices, make him gracious and turn away his anger. This God of the priests exploits human ignorance, credulity and distress.

That too is a misuse of God.

Has God helped?

'God has helped,' I read on a votive tablet hanging in a side chapel of a baroque church in Bavaria. The little picture, lovingly and naively painted on the tablet, showed a woman getting up from her sick bed.

There is no reason to laugh in intellectual superiority at the trusting faith of the person saying thank-you. Nevertheless, for the truth's sake I must ask quite simply, 'Was it really God who intervened here and made the terminally ill person healthy again? Or was it the knowledge and ability of her doctor, the power of her body to heal itself? Or just fortunate circumstances?'

'God has helped.' Anyone who speaks like this is interpreting the fact of their healing after the event as divine intervention.

'God (Allah, Yahweh, Shiva) has intervened to help me – preserved me – guided me – saved me – given me; Mary (or Isis or Artemis) has heard my weeping.' All these are interpretations, not facts.

All facts first gain their special significance through a specific interpretation. Faith interprets everything that happens in human life in terms of God. Therefore a believer can regard his or her healing as an answer by God to prayer. But as I have said, that is only a subjective interpretation, not a fact.

Does God exist?

The very universality and constancy of ideas of God in human history prevent me from dismissing the reality that we call 'God' as something that does not exist, or even denying it. The greatest thinkers in human history have wrestled with this question. There is also a denial of God which – as the theologian Wolfhart Pannenberg puts it – rests on 'intellectual barbarity'. The majority of all people on earth live, think and act out of a commitment to this reality, God, even if they give it very different names and interpretations.

Nevertheless the question remains: does what we call 'God' really exist? If I am to be able to say a Yes or a No or even a Perhaps or a Probably, first I need to know what is meant by the word 'God'. Above all I have to detach this question from the horizon of my own religion and put it in a more universal context. That makes it: Does Allah exist? Do (or did) El, Adonai, Yahweh, the biblical deities, exist? Did Marduk exist? Did Amun, Horus, Aten, Anubis, Hathor, Nut and Isis exist? Did Zeus or Jupiter, Aphrodite or Venus exist? Do Shiva, Vishnu and Brahma exist?

What am I to answer? I don't know. But to be consistent I would have to say of the biblical Christian God what I would say of the other deities, dead and still living.

There are words, images, ideas in which the whole of humankind names a last, all-supporting reality, the basic mystery of existence. The words, images and notions change; they are historically conditioned and culturally different. All ideas of God that there are or were in the religions of this earth are only approximations to this unnameable and ungraspable reality. That is also true of the Christian religion!

I dare say that even in our Western, secularized world this reality is at the centre of the thought, questioning and searching of most thinking people. Still! Only it is no longer recognized as the question of God, but as the question of existence and meaning.

But the reality which we denote with these many different names and images is really there. That I believe.

Meaning – another word for God?

The world may have a meaning. Life may have a meaning. Human existence may have a meaning. Being born may have a meaning, and also dying. I even live by the fundamental trust that the world and life have an underlying meaning which is at work in them. But I do not know this meaning. It conceals itself from me. I can only hope and trust in it, never grasp and possess it.

It is the same with God as it is with meaning. Perhaps the question of the meaning of life is identical to the question of the meaning of God. Is that why we look so hard for meaning? Meaning – is it another word for God, whom we seek, of whom we have an inkling but whom we do not recognize, who veils himself from us, whose existence we can only hope for in trust?

Or to put the question the other way round – in the same words. Is the question of God identical with the question of the meaning of life? Is that why we look for God? Is God another word for the meaning of life, which we seek, of which we have an inkling but which we do not recognize, which veils itself from us, the existence of which we can only hope for in trust?

I trust that meaning is there because I trust that God is there.

God – a person?

In the biblical religions the notion of God is bound up with the notion of a personal God who exists exalted high above human beings and the earth and from there intervenes on this earth to bring salvation or to punish, to guide and to lead in history.

Such an interpretation is completely human. For somehow biblical people had to interpret the event that the Bible reports. And what was more natural than to infer from the familiar image of a powerful human person a powerful divine person active from heaven, who hears and sees, who thinks and speaks, directs and commands, is angry and forgives?

The notion of God as a person also governs talk of God in Christianity and the church. Perhaps in fact there is no better image with which to imagine God than that of a human person. But even if I imagine God as a person and address him as 'You', I must be aware that this notion of God, too, is merely a figurative anthropomorphic projection, a crutch which our minds need in order to be able to imagine something that is really unimaginable.

Our brain has not developed any adequate forms for imagining what we call God. All the images and words that we use to denote God at best have the character of a figurative analogical approximation to what is meant, giving it vivid concrete form. The image of the person which believers and non-believers alike use when speaking of God is merely such an aid to concrete imagination.

The language of the Bible itself offers sufficient other images when it touches on the mystery of God: impersonal images like light, life, truth, way, rock, spring, cloud, salvation, heaven, etc. They are just as valid as the image of an other-worldly divine person, and at the same time just as invalid. However, they relativize the anthropomorphic image of a divine person, which has probably become the strongest image in Christian thought and language about God.

Today, it seems to me, talk of God as an other-worldly person has made it more difficult for many people to believe in God.

Ultimate concern

I can get another, perhaps more helpful, notion of what is denoted by 'God' if I do not imagine God in an anthropomorphic way under the image of an other-worldly super-person, but more from an existential aspect.

Luther remarked, 'What you set your heart on is your God.' At the same level of understanding Paul Tillich describes God as 'ultimate concern'. According to this understanding the word 'God' denotes what human beings regard as ultimately decisive and normative for well-being, success, salvation, happiness, the future and the fulfilment of their lives. Is God a name for that on which we pin everything?

The safe ground on which we can build our lives; the anchor to which we can make ourselves fast in the swirling currents of life; the support which prevents us from being swept away – faith calls it 'God'.

We look for orientation in a life of which we cannot make sense. We long to be shown the way. Where are the ways leading us? Which way is right? Who points it out to us? Faith speaks of – God.

Israel gave the name 'God' to that power from which the people hoped for the aversion of disaster, liberation from enemy oppression and deliverance from distress. And the name God also stands for the darkness which awaits us beyond the threshold of death. Where the religions promise human hope eternal life, the fulfilment of all longings and abiding salvation, they also give it the name God.

So is God a name for the mystery of the dark origin of our existence, for the unknown meaning and future of our existence which is hidden from us, for the alpha and omega of all things?

The ineffable

The Bible itself is aware of the inadequacy of its images of God. The God of the Bible is not a God who can be grasped. He refuses to give his name and as a result remains outside people's control. He hides himself in his cloak and conceals himself in the cloud. He lives in light inaccessible. Israel's prohibition against making itself an image of God is perhaps the most valid thing that human beings have ever said about God.

Although they did not know anything of what present-day evolutionary epistemology says about the conditioning of human intellectual capacity, the really great Christian thinkers were always aware of the ineffability of God, the impossibility of thinking and speaking in a valid way about God in categories drawn from the world of human experience.

Gregory of Nazianzus said: 'No words express you. How shall I name you, you whom one cannot name, you who are beyond all things? Is that not all that can be said of you?'

Augustine said: 'God cannot even be called the ineffable because that, too, says something. So it is better to keep silent.'

Anselm of Canterbury said: 'I move and am in you and yet I cannot reach you. You are in me and around me but I do not perceive you.'

Thomas of Aquinas said: 'What God really is remains hidden from us for all time, and this is the highest that we can know about God in this life: that God transcends any thought which we can think about him.'

How intolerable is the church's superior attitude when it

claims to know precisely what the truth about God is and what God wants or does not want!

'Playing with God in the kindergarten'

There was an international conference of university lecturers and professors of religious education in Salzburg. The city fathers held a reception at the Residenz. In his witty and charming speech of welcome the president remarked that he did not entirely trust pastors and teachers of religion: 'These people keep talking about God as if they had played with him in the kindergarten.'

Although this man was a politician and not a theologian, he had seen through the usual church talk of God. He had understood more about God than most of those who talk professionally about God.

The church God

I do not know what God is like. But I am fairly certain that God is not like the God whom I have encountered in the churches since my youth, the God to whom the pope and the bishops appeal, the God who is described in the catechism, the God who is invoked in the liturgy.

The biblical God could not be grasped; he kept himself to himself and constantly withdrew further; he came and went whenever he wanted, observed no rules and was always good for surprises. However, this God was captured, tamed and disciplined. He was measured, registered and catalogued. Now he can be calculated and manipulated. Now people know precisely who he is, what he can and cannot do. This church God is a domesticated God.

The church God has assumed the features of the priests of the church. He reeks of incense and has a marked preference for formal liturgies. He loves the solemn splendour of liturgical occasions and is fond of dressing himself in vestments from the cope chest in the sacristy. Above all he likes it when people do something 'in his honour'. He likes nothing better than sacrifices. These are now offered to him daily on millions of altars. When he speaks, he uses the same ceremonious, pompous and obfuscating sacral language as his priestly representatives., He shares their antipathy to the sexual, but values large families.

The church God is unfortunately not just a satire. He actually exists. I've met him often.

The language of church affairs

Perhaps I sometimes find it difficult to believe in God because my head is stuffed so full of all the sayings, formulae, images and concepts with which God is talked about in the church. Perhaps my view of God is constantly being distorted by the stereotyped phrases in the language of the preachers which have become banal clichés, by the imagery and conceptuality of liturgical language and church declarations. God is certainly there. But the language of church affairs keeps pointing me in the wrong direction. It prevents me from finding God.

Intellectual laziness

Almost every time I hear the word 'God' in church I could replace it with another word which would give a more probable explanation without saying 'God' at all. We simply say 'God' if we cannot explain something otherwise. We say 'It is God's will' when we are too lazy to investigate the causes of an event carefully and thoughtfully. The leaders of the church say 'God wills it' when their arguments are no longer convincing. They say, 'God has ordained it' when they can no longer justify and legitimate the regulations of the organization in any other way.

Usually our use of the name 'God' to interpret anything is simply the result of lazy thinking and the force of habit. The inhibitions of Jews about uttering the name of God says infinitely more about God, and in a better way, than the inflated verbosity of the church's preaching about God.

Perhaps the most important knowledge

Anyone who has spent a lifetime mastering the skills of brewing beer, practising tax law, metallurgy, bacteriology or the history of the Incas, ends up knowing a great deal about the subject. I have spent a lifetime grappling with the topic of God. And what do I know now? Nothing! Nothing at all! Except that I know that I know nothing. But perhaps that is the most important thing that one can know of God. I know that God cannot be named, cannot be comprehended or grasped and is beyond our control.

If I remember rightly, it was Albert Einstein who once remarked: 'Looking for truth is like looking in a pitch dark cellar for a black cat which probably is not there.'

Now if that also applies to the 'truth' of which the religions speak when they say 'God', what a fool I am! If only I had opened a pizzeria in my youth or learned a solid craft, instead of grappling with God!

And yet I cannot let things be.

The burden of God

In a small village in upper Austria between the Danube and the Bohemian forests the church of the small community is guarding an important work of art, a precious carved altar from the fifteenth century.

Time and again, when I am in that area, I am drawn there,
and I am always particularly impressed by the same thing: the
figure of St Christopher at the centre of the altar. Usually the
Christopher who carries the child Jesus in the legend and almost
collapses under the burden is depicted as being powerful and
muscular, rugged and bearded.

But here for the first time I met quite a different Christopher,
who opened my eyes to the deeper truth of the legend. This
Christopher is slim, almost dainty, with a slight build. His face
is gaunt, ascetic, spiritualized, marked by sorrow and resigna-
tion. He is a man of prayer who wrestles with God, a thinker
who ponders.

He carries God on his shoulders and this burden, the burden
of God, oppresses him. The unknown artist from the late
Middle Ages experienced more of the reality of God than is laid
on most believers.

I recall conversations with Fridolin Stier, who was not only a
great theologian and scholar but also a great man of piety. He
told me that Martin Buber, the famous Jewish philosopher of
religion, had once sat in the seat in which I was sitting and had
spoken with him about 'suffering from God', 'collapsing under
God', about the heavy 'burden of God'. God is also a burden,
oppressiveness, darkness, as the Bible already knows.

At that time – I was about forty – I didn't really understand
what Stier meant. Now I've got a bit further.

. . . because God really is there

The scientist Hoimar von Ditfurth points out that the fins of
fishes could only develop as they did because water offered
particular forms of resistance. Similarly, the wings of the bird
could only develop because the element of air was there; and the
eye could only be formed because there are light waves with
particular properties. He goes on to conclude that human
consciousness and thought could only develop in evolution

because there is a reality, spirit, which is objectively present (22/ 317).

If that is the case, then perhaps one could also say that religions and notions of God could only develop in human evolution because there is this reality, God.

I believe that what we call God is really there and is the reality which is closest to us, despite all the misuse of his name, despite all the limitations and narrow-mindedness of human thought and language about God, despite the caricatures of him.

So I trust that an ultimate meaning is hidden behind all the meaninglessness and behind all the nonsense; that an ultimate truth is hidden behind all the impenetrable darkness, all the errors and lies; that an ultimate goodness is present behind all the terrors that happen in this world, namely God.

God is different

I believe that there is an ineffable and unnameable reality which brings forth, permeates and embraces everything in the world: a reality which gives a meaning to everything that happens and a goal to all becoming. We give the name God to this all-embracing first and last reality which is there before, behind, over and under the reality that can be perceived; this last comprehensive meaning; this ultimate truth, this ultimate goodness, this deepest ground from which all merges, this ultimate goal towards which everything moves. What God is and how God is remains hidden from me. God is shrouded in a veil of mystery. I cannot grasp him, possess him, hold him fast. But God is there. I feel that I am held by him.

However, I doubt whether God resembles what is usually said of him in the church. I know that all this talk is anthropomorphic figurative language, but in almost all the places in which God is spoken of in the church – from ordinary sermons through episcopal pastoral letters to statements of the magisterium – these anthropomorphic images are objectivized so that they become real substantive statements. And this is where my unease begins: doubts arise, resistance stirs. I doubt whether such notions and such talk really do justice to the reality of God.

God is different.

5

Created in the beginning . . .

An unnecessary dispute

'In the beginning God created heaven and earth.' That's how the
first chapter of the Bible begins. Right down to the beginning of
this century a vigorous battle raged between church theologians
and natural scientists over belief in creation. After Darwin's
discoveries about 'the origin of species', it had become clear to
scientists that it was impossible to accept the information in the
Bible about the creation of the world and human beings.
However, the church insisted that as 'divine revelation' the
Bible cannot contain false teaching and that therefore what is
reported in it is to be accepted in faith. Today – above all
through historical criticism of the Bible – we know that this
dispute was quite unnecessary.

Nevertheless an inadequate understanding of the biblical
belief in creation is still widespread, both among scientists and
among believers in the church.

As can be seen from the new Catechism, the magisterium
of the church has not sufficiently noted and assimilated either
the insights of contemporary natural science or the results of
present-day biblical theology.

The believer is accustomed to see biblical Christian creation
faith as an answer revealed by God to our questions about the
beginning of the world and its cause. Understood in these terms,
belief in creation has also been handed down in the church for
almost two thousand years. As long as the sciences did not contradict it, this belief caused no great difficulties.

However, confrontation and controversy with the different insights of the natural sciences forced theology to seek a new and better understanding of the doctrine of creation. Biblical-Christian creation faith need not be opposed to present-day knowledge about the origin of the world, life and humankind, since it is about something quite different from the question of the beginning of the world.

The biblical texts

It has to be realized that the biblical faith in a creator God developed only relatively late within the people of Israel. Belief in Yahweh, the God who liberated Israel from Egypt, existed centuries before this God was also celebrated as creator of the world. The earliest texts in which there are the beginnings of a belief in creation in Israel are praises of God in which God is celebrated as giver and author of all good gifts, but not as creator.

The two accounts of the creation which we find at the beginning of the Bible are later. The earlier of the two accounts, the so-called Yahwistic account, is a naive and graphic narrative. It occurs in the second chapter of the book of Genesis and chronologically is assigned to the age of the so-called 'Enlightenment' under Solomon. So it may have taken literary shape around 950 BCE. That was at any rate around three hundred years after Moses and almost a thousand years after Abraham. And the so-called 'Priestly' hymn to creation which is to be found in the first chapter of the Bible is another four hundred years later. It was only composed when the Jews were living in exile in Babylon, i.e. around 550 BC.

The Bible formulated its belief in creation in competition with the creation myths of Israel's neighbouring peoples. The earlier text on the creation is modelled on Egyptian myths in many details. For example, the formation of human beings from clay has been taken from the Egyptian myth of the potter god

Chnum. The Priestly account of God's six-day work of creation serves as the foundation for the sabbath commandment. In it we find not only the Babylonian view of the world at this time but also parallels to Babylonian creation myths.

Creation stories: an interpretation of the present

Israel's belief in the creation of the world by its God Yahweh thus first came into being at a time when belief in Yahweh as deliverer, liberator, lawgiver and king of Israel had already been alive for centuries. Creation faith was not the basis for belief in God, nor did it lead to it; on the contrary, already existing belief in God produced creation faith.

The relationship to God which the people of Israel were experiencing at that time was projected back into the past. The present was interpreted and explained by a narrative about the beginnings in the past.

Like a transparency which is put into a projector and then becomes visible on a distant screen, so Israel projected its current belief by means of the narrative-hymnic depiction of a remote 'beginning' of this world. The 'beginning of the world' became a projection on a screen on which a contemporary interpretation of life became visible.

The longer I reflect on these questions, the clearer it becomes to me that creation faith cannot comprise statements about the beginning of the world. The origin of the world is not the theme of creation faith, either for the natural sciences or for religion and theology. The biblical accounts of creation are only the screen on which quite different statements about God, the world and human beings are depicted.

The topic of the creation narratives is not the historical and factual event of a distant beginning of the world and human beings, but the present-day life of human beings in the world with all its threats and hopes, with all the good and beautiful things that are experienced, all the evil and suffering to which human life in this world is exposed. In the midst of such experiences the creation narratives express Israel's trust in the nearness of its God.

The biblical belief in creation is rooted in the thanksgiving of the people of Israel to a God from whom they believed that they had received everything: freedom from forced labour in Egypt and the land in which they lived. So Israel's creation faith was really rooted in thanksgiving for concrete gifts and not in a speculation about the origin of the world. Israel's creation faith interpreted the world as one given by its God. And it gave thanks for this. Because Israel believed in a God who 'is there for us', the divine name Yahweh can be translated 'I am there for you'; Israel interpreted the world as a world which is 'there for human beings'.

The creation myths depict the relationship between Israel and its God. But they say nothing about the origin of the universe and nothing about the first human beings. Nothing at all! Everything that they say about this derives from the picture of the world current in the the ancient Near East and reflects the ignorance of that time.

The documents of the biblical creation faith which were also taken over later by Christianity are not a divine revelation of knowledge about the origin of the world and human beings but an interpretation of the world in terms of the faith experienced by Israel, an interpretation of the world with the help of myth.

The magisterium of the church finds it difficult to accept this information from its own biblical theologians and to correct the doctrinal views which have been expressed so far. The understanding of the creation myths as the revelation of knowledge about the world and human beings is a misunderstanding which arose from reading and understanding myths and hymns as factual historical accounts. That was the great error of the church, which also brought alienation between science and religion. The repudiation of the insights of Copernicus, Galileo and Giordano Bruno has its cause here.

Many people in the church think that they have to defend a

bastion of God, whereas in reality they are merely clinging to time-conditioned notions depending on a world-view in which earlier generations were once able to clothe, express and communicate their belief. Traditional thought has cemented God in these notions.

A danger to belief in God?

In his book *A Brief History of Time,* the famous physicist Stephen W. Hawking tells of a conference on cosmology which was arranged by Jesuits in the Vatican in 1981:

> 'The Pope told us that it was all right to study the evolution of the universe after the big bang, but we should not enquire into the big bang itself, because that was the moment of Creation, and therefore the work of God. I was glad that he did not know the subject of the talk I had just given at the conference – the possibility that space-time was finite but had no boundary, which means that it had no beginning, no moment of creation. I had no desire to share the fate of Galileo' (10/ 128).

This remark by the pope seems to me to be typical of the prejudice of church thought. The work of researchers and its results are always felt to be a threat to belief in God. Even now! This way of thinking has not changed essentially since the days when Giordano Bruno was burned on the Campo di Fiori and Galileo was banned from speaking.

A God who feared that progress in human knowledge and changes in our picture of the world would dethrone him would not be God. He would be an idol, devised by human brains and carved by human hands, like the old figures of gods. A pope who thinks that he has to warn scientists against getting too close to the creator God with their questions about the origin of the universe is speaking of an idol, not of God.

The God in whom I believe is not afraid of any striving of the human spirit towards knowledge. He delights in any correct knowledge, whether in the sphere of the natural sciences or in the sphere of theology. Right insights can bring people nearer to the truth, and thus also nearer to God. There is no knowledge of the truth which leads away from God. For God *is* the ultimate all-embracing truth of the universe.

The 'God of the gaps'

God is still always identified with the historical vessels in which human language and time-conditioned notions once attempted to hold him. When these ideas are put in question and corrected by progress in human knowledge, many believers see their belief in God threatened.

They have placed God in the gaps of human knowledge and ability. The famous theologian Dietrich Bonhoeffer called this God a 'God of the gaps'. As creator of the world and human beings, the God of Jewish-Christian-Islamic tradition had in fact occupied a gap from which he was difficult to displace. Human beings, oppressed by questions about where the world, life and human beings come from and what it all means are inclined to fill this unclosable gap in their knowledge and explanations with the word God: God created the world. Who else could have done such a thing? That is what the ancient peoples said in their creation myths, no matter what name they gave to God. That is what the people of the Bible also said. That is what the church has said.

And each time scientific research has succeeded in filling one of these gaps, religion has seen God in danger of being driven from the ancestral abode which he has been granted. The physicist Laplace once told Napoleon that he did not need the hypothesis of God to explain the origin of the universe. I'm afraid that he was right. Although the areas of ignorance in the relevant natural sciences are infinitely greater than those of assured knowledge, any God who was used to explain the inexplicable would be none other than the well-known 'God of the gaps'. This God, too, would have to give up his domain as creator of the world as soon as science was able to fill the gap into which hitherto the name of 'God' had been inserted. He would be a God who was condemned to withdraw to ever remoter places in constant rearguard actions. A poor God!

Time and again a God has had to be used to explain the inexplicable, to give a reason and a meaning to all life and activity, all toil and suffering. I find it increasingly difficult to believe in such a God. But that is no loss.

Room is made – for God.

The truth of creation faith

Creation faith is not a statement about a distant first beginning of the world and human beings, whether scientific or religious. It is a way in which people have expressed their belief in a God who is experienced as being present in their lives.

The first sentence in the Bible, 'In the beginning God created heaven and earth', does not refer to a temporal beginning of the universe as physics understands it. 'In the beginning' is an expression from the language of myth: it does not denote a past point in time but a present process of creative bringing forth: all that is has its living ground in God.

Creation faith is a statement about the world which is always present, in which God constantly 'happens', 'becomes', 'emerges', 'brings forth', 'becomes visible', 'is incarnate', 'is active', 'enlivens' – just as the spiritual is constantly present and active in the corporeal.

This 'interpretation of the world from faith' found its linguistic and literary expression in the creation myths. These are the vessels of belief in a God whom one can trust. Creation faith encourages us to live by trust in a God who is present in life. It articulates this basic trust with the help of mythical descriptions of the beginning.

The 'truth' which is communicated to believers in the acceptance of a creation faith does not grant us any 'revealed knowledge' about the origin of the world and human beings. It does not communicate any historical facts. Rather, it is an existential truth, a truth about the relationship between human beings and God, the world and themselves: truth about human beings, today, here and now.

One last thing: I do not see the creator God just as the one who is the cause of a 'beginning in time', thought of in terms of physics. I believe in God as creator God because I believe that the 'reality God' is present in the world today, here and now; that it underlies the totality of the world as the deepest reality. This reality embraces it, emerges in it, opens itself up, permeates it, allows it to become.

A God of becoming!

6

Complaint dismissed

The loving God

God is love. That is what the New Testament proclaims. In so
doing it also says that love is the human capacity closest to God
and emphasizes love as the real way to God, 'for love is of God,
and anyone who loves is born of God and knows God. Anyone
who does not love, does not know God, for God is love,' we
read in I John (4.8); this is a statement about God which is
regarded, probably rightly, as the great high point of biblical
ideas about God.

It is indeed a long way from the cruel, demonic deities of prehistory who had to be assuaged by human blood; from the
capricious gods of Olympus who played their arrogant games
with the dying; from the egotistic tribal god of the Hebrew
people who in the book of Joshua helps his people to devastate
the cities of the Jebusites and Canaanites, the Perizzites and the
Hittites, to that God whom Jesus trustingly addresses as Abba.

As in all the writings of the New Testament, among many
great thinkers and teachers of Christianity God appears as the
real source of love between human beings. When people love
one another – says Christian faith – something is manifested
of God, since there God is at work, disaster is overcome, and
salvation is created. I've also taught that, and perhaps it was
even the most important thing that I attempted to learn.

A *projection of basic human experiences?*

The first contours of this image of God already emerge in Judaism, especially with the prophets. Like all images of God, it is rooted in basic human experiences which are stored in the deepest levels of the soul and from there projected into notions of God.

We experience how love can heal wounds in human life, overcome evil, make peace, produce solidarity and bring happiness and fulfilment. Deeper reflection on human life can show us to what degree well-being or disaster in human life are dependent on effective love.

I can well imagine how such experiences and reflections led biblical reflection on God to attribute this love, which was experienced as bringing wholeness, to the God who was believed in, so that he was seen as the source of this love.

The origin of this image of God in the projection of basic human experiences does not detract from its meaning and greatness. Belief in a God who is love may have done an infinite amount of good in humankind and motivated countless people to love.

The origin of love?

It was almost a shock to me when in investigating behavioural research I came to realize that the 'origin of love' can also be seen in quite a different way.

Some behavioural scientists see the beginning of the human capacity for love in the evolutionary development of brood care. Among invertebrate species and the lower vertebrates social behaviour is still largely conflictual, i.e. others are seen as opponents. Among reptiles, for example, social life is governed by a tension between domination and submission. Even when courting, reptiles do not show any friendliness to each other. Only the development of the birds and mammals towards the end of the mesozoic period produced new social possibilities. With the 'invention' of brood care, the actions of care and concern came into the world, which evolution later utilized for the social bonding of adult birds and mammals. Their courting rituals contain modes of behaviour derived from the mother-child relationship, and this feature extends to human behaviour. For example, the tender billing and cooing of many birds is a ritualization of the mouth-to-mouth feeding of their young. The human kiss also belongs in this context.

> 'Brood care did not just bring the instruments of friendliness into the world. Love, too, defined as a personal bond, took its origin here. With brood care the family emerged as a new level of organization in the world. A family ethic could be developed which was transferred to the group, even to the anonymous large groupings of modern men and women . . . To a certain degree we tame the archaic conflictual impulses by this genuinely felt motivation' (6/ 29).

A rethinking

I am now torn between two possibilities of understanding the origin of love:

On the one hand, there is the great statement in I John which traces love back to the most exalted origin, to God himself, who is love and thus becomes the source of all love.

And on the other hand there is the succinct information from behavioural research which relativizes all profundity, treats it soberly and demystifies it: love has its origin in brood care. The contrast is great.

Is God again on the retreat here too? This time from the authorship of the most beautiful and the best in the world? Does it again have to be conceded that the church's usual way of thinking has made God a God of the gaps in order to interpret a mystery which hitherto escaped rational explanation?

Everything in me struggles against this suspicion. But I may not simply suppress it in order to salvage for myself a familiar notion which gives security and certainly is a grandiose one.

If what behavioural research claims is really true – and this seems to me to be quite probable – then what it says is a challenge to Christian faith to rethink theologically its talk of a loving God, to understand it more deeply and correctly, and certainly also to preach it in a different way from usual. Just as church theology was challenged by the discoveries of Copernicus and Darwin and forced to examine theologically its traditional understanding of biblical testimonies, with the result that it finally came to understand its real truth in a more valid way and to interpret it more credibly – though after a delay of some centuries – so here too belief in a loving God could be understood in a more appropriate way, which does more justice to the Bible and once again becomes credible to men and women.

Above all, this could also perhaps offer a more credible answer to the question of the oppressive contradiction between faith in a loving God and the manifest fact of the immeasurable suffering in the world which he has created.

And suffering?

Belief in a loving God was always exposed to doubt in the biblical Christian story of faith. The experience of suffering in the world is too manifest a contradiction to this image of God. This loving God has been contradicted every day since the very beginning of life on earth by the immeasurable suffering, pains and tears of its creatures.

No theodicy over which theologians greater and lesser have puzzled for millennia can bridge the abyss between the suffering in the world and a God who is described as the origin of love.

Theological excuses

All theological attempts to justify God prove in the end to be sophistries which often almost mock suffering creation, human beings and animals. Theologians can reduce the contradiction only by diminishing the weight of suffering. They talk down suffering and pain by comparing them with 'the glory which awaits us'. They defend suffering with the 'unfathomability of the divine will' and claim that the living God sends suffering only to achieve something good: God wants to test our faith, to purify us. God sends suffering – they say – to punish us for our sins and to give us an opportunity to atone for the insult that we have done to God through our guilt, and to make it good again.

When my father-in-law lay dying and was tormented with quite intolerable pain, my wife asked the sister who was looking after him to give him some pain-relieving medicine which had been prescribed by the doctor, so that he did not have to suffer so fearfully in the hour of his death. The pious woman roundly refused, saying 'We may not cut short his suffering now. He must go on doing penance for his sins. The more he suffers now, the more quickly he will get to heaven.'

And that was not just the personal view of an individual who had been misled; it was a doctrinal view widespread in Catholic piety, which was preached from the pulpit and is still widespread, especially among the clergy. Heretics were once burned with the same arguments.

Don't these pious people see at all how they are perverting the God of Jesus? No! The accusation against the 'loving God' cannot be dropped and theologized away as quickly as that. The weight of suffering in the world is too great.

Job and God

I picked up the book of Job once again and read it. Yet again the impression forced itself upon me that this great poem is one of the most important writings in the Bible and should be included among the greatest works of world literature.

The biblical Job resists the theological appeasement of his friends. He has the stronger arguments, even against God, and persists in his accusation: 'He brings the pious low like the godless. When his scourge suddenly kills, he mocks at the despair of the innocent.'

However, Job receives an arrogant rebuff from his God: 'Where were you when I founded the earth? Tell me, if you know. Have you ever commanded the morning, or determined the place of the dawn?'

Sentence by sentence God spells out his superiority. He dresses down the complainer. God makes Job feel how small a creature he is: 'How can such a miserable creature as you dare to come to me with such objections?' This God basks in his absolutism. He humiliates the suffering Job. He plays with human suffering because he wants to win the wager with Satan. If God really were as he is depicted in this book of the Bible, I wouldn't want anything to do with him. I would despise him. Job is right, not this God.

The biblical book ends in a disappointing way: Job gives in; he submits and repents: 'Therefore I have uttered what I did not understand, things too wonderful for me, which I did not know. Therefore I despise myself, and repent in dust and ashes.' And thereupon 'the Lord restored the fortunes of Job . . . and gave Job twice as much as he had before'.

Fridolin Stier, who has become famous as a translator and interpreter of Job, once told me in a conversation that this harmonizing conclusion to the book of Job was added to the book only much later. Even the Old Testament redactors of the Bible could not bear the tension of the contradiction between the suffering in the world and God. They did what all theologians do; they played down suffering. They made it clear to people that they were wrong to accuse God. That was the only way in which they could rescue God.

Pale theologies

Most theologians today still speak very much in the style of Job's God. Walter Kasper: 'One cannot judge God; one cannot want to nail down and fix his actions. God is the wholly other, the mysterious . . . God is so great that he does not need to prove his greatness at the expense of the history and order of the world' (2/139).

The fine talk of Jürgen Moltmann seems to me to be just as questionable: 'Here God's divinity and God's future is access-ible to Christian faith only in the form of the crucified. It finds in it the "suffering of God" in the world as it is, and sees in this suffering of God the passion of God for a new world' (2/142).

Those are just two voices from a choir of many. Although I have a high regard for the two theologians I have mentioned and think that they are among the really good theologians, their theodicy, too, seems to me to be pale theology. The tortuous language, which conceals more than it reveals, unmasks their helplessness in the face of the question of suffering. No theo-logian can cleanse God of guilt for the suffering of creation with sophistic arguments. If God brought forth this world, then he also brought forth the unspeakable suffering in it. Every day, including today, he has to keep his ears closed so that he does not hears the cries of pain of all those people and animals whom he causes to suffer.

Relieving God of a burden

I see only two possibilities of relieving God of the burden of the suffering of this world. The first is for us also to relieve God of the responsibility for causing this world, in other words to abandon belief in creation. Or, and that would be the second possibility, it is for us to give up faith in a loving God. A God who looks on inactively when his creatures suffer is never a loving and merciful God.

It then immediately strikes me that there is still a third possibility. There is not even a personal God. Again my often repressed suspicion arises that 'God' is merely another name for life itself; for life with all its good things, but also for life in its tragic dimension.

I once talked with a colleague who has now retired. He had been responsible in particular for religious education in school; he arranged school worship and also got involved in the local church community. He was a man of deep faith. We talked about death and what comes afterwards. I argued that all life finally ends in God. Then he quite suddenly protested vigorously: 'I don't want to end up with a God who has made this world in which there is so much suffering and misery, with a God who allows this infinite suffering and doesn't change anything.'

This passionate outburst shook me.

Suffering – woven into the structure of life

On a thoughtful reading, it struck me that all the powers of which the God of the book of Job boasts to justify his unassailable superiority rest on notions from a naive view of the world. This saw the immediate action of a God enthroned above the earth in any inexplicable event. Although the arguments are put forward in grandiose figurative ways of speaking and with poetic force, they rest on an inadequate knowledge of the actual causal connections in the world. Hardly a single one of them would stand up to critical scientific questioning today.

Only in a theistic interpretation is the book of Job an argument with God; from an existential perspective it is the argument of every suffering human being with a life shot through with suffering.

All the sufferings which came upon Job are sufferings which are woven into the structure and character of that life which has developed here on earth over many hundreds of millions of years in a particular way and not otherwise; always endangered by deficiency and need, always threatened by sickness and death; delivered over to the impersonal workings of nature, often directed by change and subject to a blind providence; constantly exposed to hostilities and conflicts; constantly oppressed by envy and disapproval; delivered over to the violence of the more powerful; woven into the power of evil around us and in us; and assailed from the depths of our own souls with their contradictory strivings.

The dynamic of the evolutionary development of life is blind to the tears which living beings have shed; it is deaf to their cry of pain. It is directed towards the survival of the species, to the general development of life. It is not interested in the well-being or disaster, the happiness or suffering, of individuals. It knows no compassion and no mercy.

No wonder that the people of the Bible created a merciful and compassionate God for themselves!

Haggling with God?

When I attempt to understand the suffering of the world in the context of physics, chemistry, biology, sociology or psychology, I can perhaps still understand it as a fact of the world with a objective basis. I can live with a fact which is simply there and which I can do nothing to change. I can become reconciled to it more easily than if I attempt to interpret the suffering in terms of God.

Although the sciences too owe me an answer to the question of the meaning of suffering, at some points they can give me an insight into over-riding connections of cause and meaning, usually more than the traditional religious answers. For example, when I learn from geology that the terrible earthquake which brought so much suffering and death to innocent human beings and animals was the result of the shifting of tectonic plates on the earth's crust, I can find a place for it more easily than if I ask helplessly, 'Why could God have allowed such a thing?' Or even, 'Why did God send this earthquake?'

If biology teaches me that pain is a warning signal from the body or that life can develop further only if it can constantly adapt itself to changed circumstances, and that a limit to the life-span of the individual is a presupposition of this, I can put even death in a meaningful context and finally recognize it as an unavoidable fact.

At all events, I can cope with it better than if I ponder questions to which I can find no answer: 'Why did God let this dear person die? Why does God make all our lives end in death? Why is the world created by God so shot through with pain?' Only if we confront the suffering in the world with belief in a loving, omnipotent God do we have hopeless haggling and questions without answers.

Complaint dismissed

The rebuff given to Job and his accusations is in fact justified, regardless of the view of the world from which it is formulated. Whether we explain it in terms of the view of God current in the ancient Near East or today's rationalistic sciences, the answer remains the same over all times and world-views: there is no point in accusing. What you accuse, whether it is God or the character of earthly life, is always greater and more powerful than you are. Faced with this super-power, you are nothing. You haven't a chance. Even your legitimate arguments don't count. The complaint is dismissed.

The impossibility of accusing God which the book of Job emphasizes is the impossibility of accusing life itself. We cannot judge, either God or the life into which we are born.

The only thing that we can do is to attempt to diminish and assuage suffering as much as possible in the little sphere in which we live. And that would be fully in accord with Jesus' instructions.

7

Revealed by God?

'. . . because God has revealed it'?

Anyone who has doubts about the truth of individual church doctrines, and asks whether what is taught by the church is really true and has to be believed, will probably be told that God 'in his infinite goodness and wisdom' has revealed it in this way and no other. It is attested in the Bible in this way and no other, and what is in the Bible is revealed by God and therefore true.

The Catechism of the German bishops states: 'God has revealed himself to us in the Old Covenant through the patriarchs and prophets and in the New Covenant through Jesus Christ and the apostles. God has spoken to us to tell us who he is and what he does, what we are and what we are to do. He has communicated to us truths which otherwise would have been hidden from us for ever.' 'What God has revealed he has proclaimed to us through the church' (11/ no.4).

This understanding of revelation is the basis of the claim of the pope and the bishops to be the infallible guardians and stewards of truth: God has revealed it like this and entrusted it to the church. So what the church teaches is true. It comes from God.

Any objection must fall silent in the face of the logic of this argument. For who would want to insinuate that God could err and give false information to the biblical authors through his Holy Spirit? There remains only the suspicion that the church could have erred in its interpretation of the Bible. But that cannot be the case either! For 'in order to preserve the church in the purity of the faith handed on by the apostles, Christ willed . . . to confer on her a share in his own infallibility' (1/ no.889).

'Mindful of Christ's words to the apostles . . . the faithful receive with docility the teachings and directives that their pastors give them in different forms' (1/ no.87).

The traditional understanding

Communicated by the customary forms of preaching and teaching and also by official church documents, the notion is prevalent among most believers that a God existing beyond the world, the creator of the world and human beings, one day almost four thousand years ago, in a small oriental people which he had chosen specially for the purpose, began to give humankind knowledge of himself.

Although our earth had already been in existence for at least four billion years and human beings had been asking about the divine at the latest since the development of their consciousness some hundreds of thousands of years previously, until then this God had kept himself largely concealed and preferred to remain unknown. He had indicated only a little about himself: through the visible world around us, through the miraculous order which prevails everywhere, as the Catechism says.

And for the rest of humankind, who were not among the elect recipients of the biblical revelation of God, there has been no more than this 'natural revelation', right down to the present day. The religion of the other peoples are therefore inferior to the biblical religion; only 'traces' of the divine have been recognized in them.

God communicated himself by intervening in history; he liberated and rescued his people, helped them to conquer their enemies and led them into a land 'flowing with milk and honey'. In this way he indicated that he was a God who guided the way of his people into a better life by caring for them, protecting them and delivering them. He is a God who is just and gracious at the same time, who punishes evil and rewards good; a God on whom one can build.

And he revealed himself by speaking to his chosen people. A majority of believers up to the higher ranks of the clergy still accept this quite literally, as I have discovered. Many people still uncritically and naively imagine that God spoke one day to Abraham, to Moses, to the prophets, with a voice that they could hear acoustically, or at least with an 'inner voice'.

In order to reveal himself, God also commissioned particular people, for example Moses and the prophets, to speak 'in his name'. He enabled them to do this 'through his Spirit which came upon them'. They became 'God's mouthpiece', and what they proclaimed was 'God's Word'. Moreover he sent angels to people to communicate messages to them.

'When the time was fulfilled', God then finally sent his only-begotten Son on earth so that he could 'give people news of the Father'. And as according to the prologue of the Gospel of John this Son of God was even pre-existent in God as the 'Word', he could 'bear witness to the truth' and reveal God through his teaching and through his life.

He entrusted his teaching to his apostles. So that they should 'abide in the truth', after his resurrection and ascension he sent them the 'Holy Spirit'. This not only illuminated the apostles and the authors of the New Testament writings; it also guides and illuminates the successors of the apostles, the pope and the bishops... down to the present day.

This, or something similar, is a description, in broad outline, of the understanding of faith prevalent among believers and currently taught.

A *historically conditioned model of understanding*

In this traditional church understanding, revelation is seen as a process which begins from a 'plan' of the creator of the world to communicate to human beings something about himself and his purposes and to give them specific instructions which will lead to their salvation. God then realized this plan by making known, in a limited period, in a limited region of the Near East, to a limited number of people, things which otherwise would have been hidden from humankind. In such an understanding of revelation the static view of the world with its hierarchical structure from above downwards is preserved, along with the naive belief in miracles held in past times.

I must honestly confess that I can no longer make much of this understanding of revelation. I too certainly believe that a historical revelation of God underlies Christian faith, but I doubt whether what we call 'revelation' really happened as it is described in the traditional preaching and instruction of the church. I see this model originating in the time-conditioned ideas and ways of thinking of the ancient world and the Middle Ages. But I can also see why the official church maintains this understanding of revelation so unerringly: it ensures that the church has exclusive possession of truths about which no further questions can be asked, because they are of direct divine origin.

Among people whose thinking is shaped by the modern picture of the world, the church's appeal to a divine revelation of its teachings is increasingly coming up against incomprehension, scepticism and repudiation. It is becoming a hindrance to faith. Therefore many theologians today see and interpret revelation in quite a different way.

I assume that what the traditional theology of the church's magisterium – thinking from above downwards – describes as a miraculous historical act of God's revelation is in reality a quite normal and natural process in the development of religious ideas, which took place and still takes place all over the world, at all times and in many ways.

We simply have to reverse the direction of our thought and ask questions from below, from human experiences, about the origin of such 'revealed truths'. That will make what 'revelation' means in Christian faith not only clearer but also more credible.

Revelation – how did it happen?

Time and again I have read in theological literature that revelation has taken place by historical people 'experiencing' God – the people of Israel in the history of its liberation from Egypt, in the settlement, in the history of its kings and prophets – and that the decisive experience of God took place through the person of Jesus.

I took over this theological information for myself and taught it for many years without further questions. I didn't perceive how woolly this way of talking is until one day some one asked me for more details. The question perplexed me, and forced me to enquire more precisely how this 'experience' of God could have taken place in particular historical situations.

Revelation – what really happened? How did it happen? How did the people of the Bible arrive at the belief that God had revealed himself to them? Through miracles? Through unusual events? Did they hear him or see him? Did he appear to them? Or did he inculcate revelation into them in a miraculous way through reflection and writing? Through his spirit?

Israel's fundamental experience of God

It is generally agreed by biblical theologians that the decisive and fundamental historical experience from which Israel's bond to the God of Moses arose was the famous deliverance at the Sea of Reeds (not the Red Sea, as it is often wrongly called). For the faith of Israel, the deliverance of the fleeing Hebrews from the pursuing troops of Pharaoh was the fundamental act of God's revelation. 'The Lord drove back the sea by a powerful east wind' (Ex.4.21). The Israelites could go through the dried-out, shallow branch of the Sea of Reeds, and their pursuers perished as the waters flowed back.

Probably the narrative has a historical nucleus. About twelve miles north of present-day Suez, a caravan route led over a ford through a Sea of Reeds which occasionally was so dried out by the east wind that herds of cattle could go through it. Thus this was a quite normal occurrence, with a natural explanation, and not a miraculous intervention by a God from the beyond.

However, for the Israelites who had been delivered, this local episode, which has been repeated a thousandfold in other ways in world history, became the occasion for centuries of praise: 'I will sing to Yahweh; he is highly exalted. The horse and rider he has cast into the sea' (Ex.19.1).

And the greater the chronological distance from the event, the more the divine intervention is decorated and heightened to make it more grandiose and miraculous. The water, which in the earlier texts only 'withdrew', later stood 'like a wall'.

Those who were delivered at the time could not see the natural causation which led to the fortunate chance of their deliverance. How else were they to interpret their experience than through the powerful intervention of the God who led them out of Egypt? In the deliverance at the Sea of Reeds God himself became manifest for them.

. . . through miracles?

Biblical faith appeals to historical experiences of the people of Israel. Israel interpreted events from its history as a miraculous saving intervention by its God. In such events Israel's God became manifest. In the original context, 'miracle' simply means that an event is interpreted as an 'act of God', as the saving intervention of Yahweh. 'Miracle' does not mean that extraordinary events took place which could only have come about through a 'supernatural' intervention by a God who did miracles.

Everything in the Bible which is described as the action of a God who reveals himself can also be seen and interpreted quite normally in human and natural terms. Even where the Bible relates miraculous and extraordinary things, we need not resort to miracles performed by God to understand it. These are contained in types of literary account which are well known to biblical critics: elaborations which heighten and exaggerate, legends and sagas which embroider, cultic praises, the poetic development of historical reminiscences, personifications of inscrutable causal connections.

So the events in which God revealed himself were not extraordinarily miraculous; they were quite normal, natural, historical events which were interpreted by quite normal people as the experience of a God who was with them, who led them and delivered them.

This is the way in which the 'experiences of God' which were the basis for the faith of Israel and were recorded in the Bible may have taken place in history. What faith today calls 'revelation' is grounded in these interpretations.

Interpretation of experiences

Did the God of the Hebrews send Joseph his dreams when he was in Egypt? Dreams and the interpretations of dreams are a popular literary stylistic means in the Bible. Were the plagues which came upon Egypt sent by this God? Such plagues keep appearing in Egypt and have natural causes. That the plagues were sent to the Egyptians by the God of Israel as a punishment is merely a later subjective and collective interpretation on the part of Israel.

Did the God whom Abraham worshipped really say to him, 'Go out?' It was probably the quite normal pressures of a nomadic existence which led Abraham and his clan to leave their homeland in Chaldaea. The later interpretation of the emigration of Abraham as an event brought about by God then came to be expressed in the anthropomorphic formula, 'God said, Go out!'

Were the Ten Commandments really dictated to Moses by Yahweh, the God of Israel? Did God appear in thunder and lightning on Sinai? Quite the reverse: this description serves to provide a later, secondary authorization of the laws and ordinances of Israel by attributing them to an act of revelation by God.

Did Job really dispute with God? When Jesus was baptized in the Jordan did God's voice really ring out from the clouds? No human being anywhere has ever heard God speak with an acoustically perceptible voice, neither Adam nor Eve, nor Noah nor Abraham, nor Moses nor the prophets. Everywhere, whether in the Old Testament or in the New, the expression 'God said' is a metaphorical phrase by which people interpreted an event as God's intervention.

Was it God who made manna fall from heaven in order to provide food for his people on their wanderings through the wilderness? Quite the contrary: the Israelites unexpectedly found saving nourishment in the edible clumps of manna which form from excretions of the tamarisk after an insect bites it, and interpreted this fortuitous event as an act of their God. Revelation?

Was it really God who chose David and had him anointed king by prophets? Or did this account interpret David's seizure of the throne after the event as the will of God? Was it meant to provide a basis and sacral confirmation from God for the rule of David and his successors?

Did God speak through the mouth of prophets? Quite the reverse: prophets spoke words which were interpreted by the tradition as the 'word of God'. No God guided the styli of the authors of the Old Testament writings. Quite the reverse: the many different texts which grew together into the Bible over almost a millennium were interpreted by people as the 'revelation of God'.

Here too, what is now called 'revelation of God' was originally a series of interpretations of historical experiences after the event from the perspective of a people who saw their history guided by a God; they were not miraculous events brought about in a 'supernatural' way.

Interpretations which have become important for humankind

These interpretations which Israel's faith found and described in the Bible became important for belief in God and were influential in the future. In them truth about God, human beings and the world was disclosed. Truth about God and humankind was not 'revealed' in miraculous events, divine voices and mysterious communications; rather, a 'truth' dawned on human beings, quite normal people, who were attempting to interpret what happened in the history of the people and their own experiences of life, and in this way were able to arrive at an abiding meaning, going beyond a particular historical situation.

Although these interpretations served limited interests, restricted to the people and the individual, and were part and parcel of what was still a very primitive picture of the world, stuck in a magical and mythical way of thinking, nevertheless they contain truth about the world and human life. This is so profound, concentrated and universal that time and again the interpretations have drawn and persuaded people of all nations, periods and world-views.

The interpretations of the Bible disclose something of our 'ultimate concern', that on which human well-being and disaster depend. In them something of a deeper truth about human beings and the world is disclosed. So even now, when reading these texts I still find truth and direction, promise and judgment – God.

To this degree they are experiences of God. To this degree they are revelation – also for us today.

Experiences of God

I want to attempt to approach the understanding of 'revelation' from below, i.e. inductively, from human experiences.

There are events, usually quite ordinary and only rarely

extraordinary, in which we suddenly become conscious of a deeper truth of life. This can compel us to correct our attitudes and can shed new light on the way that we have to follow to God. There are experiences, often bitter and seldom pleasant, which make us realize what is most important in life, what is really worth striving for.

There are encounters with people in which something dawns on us that can change our lives and give them a new direction. Sometimes relationships develop to people and ties to communities in which our life can gain support, meaning and confidence. There are moments in which one discovers a meaningfulness which points beyond the immediate moment.

There are actions which can demonstrate how hatred and enmity can be ended, evil overcome and peace gained. There are experiences which can make it clear how human life can find salvation or meet with disaster.

Words can be said which heal wounds, give hope and help us to interpret experiences, facts and events in quite a new way and find a place for them in life. As though touched by a magician's wand, we then suddenly see many things quite differently. Our attitude to the world and life is changed, and our action is shaped in quite a new way.

We may probably find the key to what the church tradition means by 'revelation' in such natural processes as the assimilation of human experience and an increase in knowledge. I recall Karl Rahner saying that theology is anthropology in disguise.

I suspect that what is described as 'revelation' in the church tradition is simply the interpretation of quite normal experiences in religious language and religious ideas. In that case all statements about God would be unrecognized statements about human beings and their existence in the world, statements which have been projected on to an other-worldly person.

'He brought something of God to earth'

On the way home from a conference we were listening to Mozart's Clarinet Concerto on the car radio. The sound of the instrument surrounded us. In the midst of the fast, aggressive traffic on the motorway a calm stole over us and we relaxed. All at once, in the middle of the noise and hustle, there was stillness, inner stillness.

My companion, a well-known theological writer, mentioned an article by Karl Barth in which Barth said that the angels in heaven play Mozart's music. I knew this remark but had forgotten its precise wording. It had stuck in my memory the other way round, not ascending, but descending. So after some thought I said: 'I don't believe that that's right. Angels didn't bring Mozart's music from earth to heaven. It was precisely the opposite. Mozart is the music of the angels. Mozart has listened to them. Mozart has brought it down from heaven to earth and enabled people to hear it. He has brought something of God down to earth.'

'He has brought something of God down to earth.' What I had said there, spontaneously adopting the almost mythical language of the quotation from Barth, is also said of someone else, Jesus. But I only became aware of that later. Isn't it blasphemy to mention Mozart's music and Jesus' message in the same breath, as a revelation of God? Not to my mind. The differences lie predominantly in the different levels and are more a matter of degree. In his little book on Mozart, Hans Küng remarks 'how wafer-thin is the boundary between music . . . and religion'. 'For both, though they are different, direct us to what is ultimately unspeakable, to mystery.' And he quotes Adorno, 'When I hear great music, I believe that I know that what this music says cannot be untrue' (14/ 33).

Great music can 'reveal' truth, truth about human beings and their 'ultimate concern'. Music can open up depths in people which touch on the very meaning of human existence. Music can give comfort to sufferers, hope to the desperate, confidence to the anxious. Music touches on a dimension of existence which we can call God.

I am now beginning to understand how, when they listened to the comfort, promise or even reprimand spoken by the prophets, the people of the Bible could say, 'These words were God's words to us. God has spoken to us.'

I am beginning to see the biblical experience of God and revelation as the extension of such experiences.

Revelation of God through Jesus?

And now I can also understand how people came to say of Jesus that they had experienced God in their encounters with him, that in him truth about God and human beings had dawned on them, that he had made God visible to them, and therefore that he had revealed God to them.

Although we can only make inferences about the historical Jesus indirectly from the New Testament witnesses, it is becoming abundantly clear that something must have emanated from this man from Nazareth which had a liberating influence on the people who encountered him. He could remove anxiety, give hope, and arouse a readiness for love, mercy and reconciliation.

In what he said it was possible to recognize another God than the God of whom the scribes and priests spoke, a God to whom one could entrust oneself, like a child to a father. Trust in him changed one's life. It was as though one began a 'new life', a life which drew on 'God', on 'truth'. He stood by his truth to his end on the cross. But his death did not end the effect that he had. Time and again down the centuries valid truth about human beings and human life has become manifest in an encounter with him – God.

And it is precisely this that traditional religious language calls the revelation of God through Jesus Christ. I can no longer imagine the revelation of God through Jesus Christ consisting in a God beyond this world devising a plan to send his Son to earth, where he is to found a church to which he communi-cates hitherto hidden, eternal, divine truths which he entrusts to it.

It must have been different! Human beings expressed and developed the way in which Jesus had affected them with the help of such figurative notions. It is possible to go along with their interpretations only in the context of such a historically-conditioned language game.

When people of that time said of Jesus, 'God has spoken through him, God has revealed himself through him, Jesus is the way, the truth and the life', they were using words, notions, images and concepts to interpret the activity of Jesus which were already there in their Jewish-Hellenistic world and which also determined their own thought. How else could they have understood them and expressed them at that time?

However, in the language of the church's magisterium these historically conditioned, figurative formulae were transformed into objectifying definitions and historical facts.

. . . *where people arrive at the truth about their lives*

What was manifested? In the writings of Max Seckler, the well-known fundamental theologian from Tübingen, I found an answer to this question which helped my understanding of revelation. What was revealed was not a hidden knowledge of a mysterious God whose cards human beings can at last see, nor a secret knowledge of the priestly caste, nor doctrinal state-ments and dogmas, nor 'eternal truths'. One cannot learn what was revealed like the rules of orthography or even like the clauses of the catechism. One can learn its truth only if one commits one's existence to it.

Revelation is not enlightenment about God. What became manifest in Jesus was, rather, truth about human beings, about their life, about the way that they are to go, about what is truly important and decisive for them. Revelation does not give me definitive knowledge about God; revelation leads me to an understanding of myself, to an encounter with my 'ultimate concern'.

Revelation happens wherever human beings arrive at the truth of their lives. Wherever something dawns on people that is truly good, right, meaningful and whole, that points the way, supports life and gives hope, revelation takes place. At the same time something can be experienced of what the Bible calls 'God', though in very differing degrees of concentration and depth.

Creation and revelation

The reality which brings forth everything, supports everything and permeates everything, that we call 'God', did not just reveal itself in particular events of biblical history; God constantly opens himself up everywhere. Something of God can be experienced and perceived in all that is and happens. God surrounds us like the air that we breathe and that keeps us alive. God comes forth like water from the underground spring which permeates the ground. 'For in him we live and move and have our being' (Acts 17.28).

Creation and revelation are not two different historical events. Creation and revelation are merely two different perspectives and interpretations of one and the same thing: the world, in which human beings live and in which God is present.

No unique event

So today I no longer see revelation as a unique historical process which – brought about by the initiative of a God – began at some point with Abraham (c. 1800 BC) and was concluded at the end of the first Christian century with the death of the last apostle. Nor can revelation be limited geographically to the area of the Near East.

Revelation is an event which takes place always and every-where, at all times, in all cultures, in all peoples, among all human beings. Revelation has taken place since human beings have been capable of asking about the meaning, foundation and goal of their lives and assimilating experiences by thinking about them. Down to the present day! Nor is revelation limited to experiences of God which have found literary expression in the Jewish and Christian Bible.

We do not find God's word only in the instructions of the Decalogue and the angry words of the prophets; in the resigned wisdom of Koheleth/Ecclesiastes; in the Sermon on the Mount and the parables of Jesus; or in the letters of Paul. We can also hear God speaking in all the great texts of human history which express what is ultimately valid for human beings and the world, and is ultimately binding on them. In them, too, human beings at all times have perceived God's word. Human beings have also been able to hear God's word in the books of judg-ment from ancient Egypt, in the teachings of the Buddha, the Hindu Vedas and the surahs of the Qur'an.

Is the difference between the writings of the Bible and the sacred scriptures of other religions qualitative? Are there really such differences of divine revelation? Is the God who is praised in Akenaten's Hymn to the Sun really a different God from the God whom St Francis celebrates in his Hymn to the Sun?

Is the experience of God which has been set down in the Bible really absolutely superior to the experience of God in other scriptures? At best I recognize different degrees of transparency, different cultural interpretations and different historical developments.

However, where the divine is concerned there are also differ-ences in degree, effectiveness and 'reliability' within the biblical literature. There are vast gaps between the 'revelation quality' of the endless casuistic enumerations of laws and precepts with often inhumane threats of punishment in the book of Leviticus and the 'revelation quality' of the discourses of Jesus in the Gospel of John. Even the texts which we find in the Bible and which therefore are regarded as the 'word of God' often only found their way into the Bible by chance, and sometimes it was also a matter of chance that others were not included.

And where are we to locate the fundamental difference between texts from the canonical holy scriptures of the religions and the texts of the universal great religious literature from all the centuries, say between the Revelation of John and Dante's *Divina Commedia*? Where is the boundary to be drawn between Job's dispute with his friends and the Dialogues of Plato, between the Song of Songs in the Bible and Shakespeare's Sonnets? All boundaries are fluid.

Boundaries are laid down only as a result of 'social agreements'. They correspond to the need of all groups with convictions to emphasize the superiority of their own teaching to others and to mark themselves off from other groups.

Certainly God also becomes word in the worlds of all who love, in the words of all who forgive, comfort and raise up. God addresses us, and thus becomes 'word' in any human being who needs our help. In all our daily life and in our encounters with others we can feel that we are being addressed by God.

In the language of love

I know that many theologians who have been stamped by the conventions of the church will now object, 'What is left of the uniqueness and unsurpassibility of the revelation of God in Jesus Christ?'

The church's teaching about the uniqueness and unsurpassibility of a revelation of God in Jesus Christ first comes home to us if we understand this formula in the language of love. Lovers can rightly say of those they love that these individuals are unique and, as far as they are concerned, unsurpassable. Such language expresses the special character that those who are loved are given by the love which singles them out. Saint-Exupéry described that in his *Little Prince* in terms of the meaning that a single rose is given when we pick it out of a field of one hundred thousand roses. In the context of such talk, the Christian faith can therefore say of Jesus that for it, he is unique and unsurpassable.

In the language of a love which makes a choice, I can still say that Jesus of Nazareth is unique, unsurpassable and decisively binding for me. For me, he has become the truth on which I have attempted to orientate my thought, despite all the errors in which I am trapped. For me, he has been the way I have attempted to follow, despite all the wrong turnings that I have taken. And he is still normative for me today. I do not know anyone else to whom I could entrust myself like this.

But church dogmatic theologians rarely speak in this 'language of love'. Very few of them understand it. They have not been taught this way of speaking. When they use these words they mean something else, an exclusive claim to 'revealed truth'. I do not simply regard the way in which the magisterium emphasizes that the biblical revelation is absolutely unique and final as an excusable expression of the human tendency to make the traditions of one's own group more binding. It is also a self-interested argument. For only a final, unique and complete revelation gives the church the claim to possess unique and unsurpassable divine truths. And only that ensures it the role of the unique and indispensable mediator between human beings and God.

8

The misunderstood images

Did it really happen as the Bible says?

At a school reunion I met an old friend whom I hadn't seen for many years. He had a doctorate in physics and now held a top post in an atomic research organization. We spoke of our schooldays and our life afterwards. When I told him that I was working in the church, was particularly occupied with religious education, and had also written some books, he looked at me with surprise. 'Now be quite honest,' he said, 'do you really believe that sort of thing?' 'Of course,' I replied, 'otherwise I wouldn't be doing this work.'

The expression on his face was midway between unbelieving scepticism and amused toleration. 'Do you really believe, then, that God created the world in six days and that Adam and Eve were the first human beings? Do you really believe the story of old Noah and his ark which he loaded with two of every kind of animal? Do you really believe that God appeared somewhere and spoke with people? Do you really believe the fairy tales about miracles which are told in the Bible? Do you really believe that Mary conceived a child by the Holy Spirit? Poor thing! And all that stuff about angels and the devil? Do you really believe that Jesus walked over the sea and that he turned water into wine and multiplied loaves? Do you believe that? And do you believe that Jesus clambered out of the grave again and then later sailed off in the direction of heaven?'

My school friend had spoken passionately. It took me several attempts before I succeeded in interrupting him, to tell him that he had completely the wrong view of the Bible stories: 'They're mostly pictorial accounts, often legends and descriptions using mythological expressions.' He interrupted my attempt to explain and said triumphantly, 'Aha, so you don't believe them either! Just tell your bishop that it's all pictures, legends and myths. He'll throw you out! As far as I know, the church teaches that it all happened as the Bible says.'

In his last remark my school friend was certainly right once again, at least as far as the traditional and official teaching of the church authorities is concerned. I couldn't blame him, since he had no inkling that in the meantime a quite different understanding of the character of biblical language had become established.

Truth – preserved in the language of images

For a long time now, biblical critics have known that the biblical texts are not records of historical events and factual accounts in the modern sense. Although historical events and facts certainly also underlie the biblical accounts, it is not the intention of the biblical authors to communicate knowledge of historical events and facts; they want to hand on biblical people's experience of God.

The 'form-critical' investigations of biblical scholars have long made it clear that the Bible expresses, preserves and hands down its experiences of God predominantly in the language of images. In so doing it makes use of forms of language and description like myths and miracle stories, legends, folk tales and sagas, dreams, the appearances of angels and visions.

. . . like a liberation

When almost thirty years ago I made the acquaintance of biblical criticism through my semi-scholarly work in the

Catechetical Institute, I found that the understanding of the Bible that it gave me was like a liberation. For so many events reported by the Bible had often seemed to me to be very improbable. I had found it too difficult for my faith to regard them as real events.

And now many of these difficulties had been removed. To believe as a Christian I no longer needed 'firmly to hold it to be true' that an angel appeared to the Virgin Mary to tell her that the Holy Spirit would come upon her and that she would bear a child.

Nor did the heavenly host which sang their song of praise over the shepherds' fields any longer cause difficulties for my faith, since I now knew that these images and legends presented post-Easter belief in the Messiah.

I was no longer compelled to defend to myself and my audience that Jesus 'as Son of Almighty God' had the power and capacity to walk on the water, to multiply loaves, to turn water into wine, to open the eyes of people who had been born blind, to recall the dead to life. I now knew the origin of all these motifs with which the Gospels painted their pictures of Jesus. And I no longer needed to imagine the resurrection of Jesus as a dead man coming to life again and rising from the tomb, after forty days to rise from the earth and to disappear in the clouds.

Nor did I need to maintain against all probability that a flood once covered the whole earth and that only Noah and his ark were saved, that the many languages of the world had come into being through the building of the Tower of Babel, or that God had handed over the tablets of the Law to Moses on Mount Sinai in lightning and thunder.

Knowledge of the literary genres of the biblical texts at that time made it possible for me to assent intellectually to Christian faith while using all my critical faculties. Many difficulties which had been created by my need for intellectual honesty had fallen away.

Had I had to go on regarding the biblical accounts as facts, as historical facts and events which had really happened, at best I

could have held on to my faith bravely and with loyalty to
the church, but with my eyes closed to all the manifest
improbabilities.

The recognition that the Bible expresses the interpretation of
its experience of God in images, legends, miracle stories or
myths made it more possible for me to gain access to the truth
that it seeks to convey.

Similar images in different religions

The images in which the Bible expresses and communicates its
experience of God mostly derive from the experience and ideas
of the ancient East. But some of them have been taken over
from the religious myths of neighbouring people and transformed. That explains the surprising similarity of many biblical
accounts to images and myths from other religions of the
ancient Near East and the Hellenistic world.

However, we also find similar images in religions which at
that time had no contact with the biblical religions, for example
in the Far East and early America. So we may conjecture
that the images and myths which are common to the different
religions have a common origin. They are much older than the
Bible and go back to the earliest archaic forms of religious
thought.

Eugen Drewermann interprets this common origin of the
images in which the religions speak of the divine in terms of
depth psychology. He sees their origin in archetypal images
which are based on the deepest strata of the human soul and are
part of the universal human heritage of all peoples.

Images which preserve life

Some information which I have gained from evolutionary biology and behavioural research could perhaps explain the origin
of such archetypal images.

The well-known Dutch zoologist Nikolaus Timbergen, who later won the Nobel prize along with Konrad Lorenz, made an illuminating experiment in the middle of the 1950s. With reels, he attached cruciform shapes made of black cardboard on a line strung high over a meadow where new-born chickens were looking for food. As soon as the chickens saw the black silhouettes above them, they rushed around in wild panic and fled.

No hen had previously had any opportunity to 'teach' the chickens the danger posed by a bird of prey. Their flight had been prompted by the image of a bird of prey. It was genetically stored in their heredity. They had not acquired the image of the enemy by individual learning; the 'species' had learned it as a whole. And what countless generations of hens had learned, usually from bitter experience, had been stored as an image in the hereditary information of their descendants in order to preserve their lives (cf. 22/ 87).

In an analogous way, images are also stored in human heredity which have not been acquired either individually or culturally. They derive from primeval experiences of humankind and have been handed down genetically.

Such experiences were important for coping with life and developing it in subsequent generations. They helped to preserve life and the species. Therefore they had to be handed on. Evolution does not leave to individual learning processes the control of behaviour which is of great importance for the survival of the species. It is entrusted to the whole species and stored genetically. This process is well known in evolutionary biology.

The information which is important for life has been stored in the biological heredity of the whole species and as a result can be handed down genetically from generation to generation. As with Timbergen's chickens, it has been stored as images in the chromosomes of the cells of our bodies in the spiral DNA chains and handed down in human generations over the millennia.

Such experiences stored as images have come down to us from a grey prehistory, from the different early stages of the development of human consciousness. They are still active in our individual behaviour, evaluation and thought. Behavioural research and depth psychology give numerous examples of this.

Archetypal primal images in the religions

The biological imprinting of images important to survival on the genetic code as depicted above could be a key to understanding those images which underlie religious language.

The images in the human soul which arise in folk tales, dreams, myths and religions are also based on experiences which were already had in the primeval period of the human race, experiences of success and failure in life, experiences of what preserves and enhances life, or what threatens and destroys it. At all times they arise from the depth of the soul and among all peoples: in dreams and folk tales, in sagas and legends, in painting and poetry, in myths and also . . . in the religions.

There are images of the powerful royal ruler, the gracious father, or the capricious despot who has to be assuaged by sacrifice. In the depths of the soul lie the images of the 'pure virgin' who can redeem from the snares of guilt; of the virgin who conceives, from whose womb the divine enters the world; of the fertile, life-giving Great Mother; and also of the comforting, compassionate 'Mater dolorosa' who knows about all the pains of this world.

The images of the youthful bringer of salvation, liberator and redeemer, the experienced guide and leader, the healing miracle-worker and the knowledgable teacher, the images of one who conquers evil and is victorious over death, all have an effect on the human soul.

The images which emerge in many myths and religions, of dying deities who descended into the underworld, arose from the dead to new, transformed life, and again returned to their divine origin, derive from experiences of changes of vegetation in the annual cycle of nature. Vegetation dies off in the autumn, and goes through the winter 'buried' in the dark earth until new life revives in the spring. These images reflect basic human experiences of life. They express the hope that all death will be transformed into new life.

Such archaic images lie deep in our souls and in the common heritage of all human beings and cultures. In them experiences of salvation and disaster, of truth and meaning, indeed of the divine, are handed down in humankind.

These are the images in which religions attempt to say what cannot be said. They are the curtains with which the religions veil the holy of holies. They provide the hewn stone from which the religions build their temples. They are the threads from which the religions weave the fabric of their myths.

Here the Jewish-Christian biblical tradition is no exception. Certainly the images from the universal heritage of humankind also underlie biblical talk of God. We find them in all the writings of the Old Testament and also of the New.

Even with such central Christian doctrines as those of the incarnation of God, the divine sonship of Jesus, his conception through the Spirit and his birth from the womb of a virgin, his miracles, his saving sacrificial death, his resurrection and ascension, we must reckon with the possibility that the significance of Jesus has been expressed and described in images which are much older than the Gospels and come from the heredity of humankind.

Disturbing faith?

An exegete friend of mine, who lectures in a seminary for priests and has written some well-known books, accepted an invitation from a convent in a neighbouring diocese to give a series of lectures to the nuns about the miracles of Jesus. Among other things he had told them that the New Testament authors had transformed Old Testament quotations into miracle stories in order to use them to proclaim Jesus as the promised Messiah, and that therefore some miracle stories do not report actual events or historical facts. As far as I know, he had also pointed out that the miracle of the wine at the marriage feast in Cana has analogies in the Hellenistic mysteries of Dionysus. The shock that this caused the good sisters, who in faith had devoted their lives to serving sick people, was so great, and their indignation so strong, that he had to break off his lecture series.

I can understand the sisters' reaction. Those who have been shaped by the understanding of faith which still prevails in the official preaching of the church will see the grounds of their faith predominantly in events which really took place in the miraculous way reported in the Bible. 'For as the Word of God, the Bible does not lie and does not err. The Holy Spirit has preserved it from that.'

'And if it all really didn't happen like that,' I have continually heard people saying, 'then nothing's true; we might as well abandon our whole faith.' I've often found it difficult to contradict the psychological logic of this argument.

Reliable foundations?

Anyone who wants to build a house looks for firm ground in which to dig its foundations. Those who entrust themselves to faith also look for firm ground on which they can build. Certainly the act of faith as a trusting reliance on God is and remains a wager, and there are no absolute certainties on which it can rely. Nevertheless, the venture of faith also requires reasons which make the venture meaningful.

Those who want to believe, seek reliable foundations which do not give way when weight is put on them. They seek supports which will bear their faith when burdened by tribulation. And they think that they can best find this firm ground which guarantees the certainty of faith in 'fixed and immovable facts', in 'historical events which actually happened'.

The human need to ground one's faith in 'firm facts' is probably the reason why many believers become vigorously defensive when they hear that many accounts in the Bible do not depict historical events but are 'pictures', even legends and myths. They feel that their faith is threatened. They are afraid that they are losing certainties which have supported their faith, and they instinctively resist this.

Myths have become facts

The church is aware of the human anxiety about taking risks, and knows how the heart seeks reliable certainties. That also applies to faith. Therefore it is ready to satisfy this longing. It is ready to offer certainties even when these are only apparent certainties.

Unimpressed by the knowledge of the church's theologians, the magisterium therefore insists on the historicity and facticity of the biblical accounts. It instinctively refuses to recognize important biblical accounts as images, myths or legends. One only has to look into the Catechism of the Catholic Church, which almost completely ignores all the results of biblical criticism and throughout its argument acts as if the imagery in the Bible depicted historical facts.

The church cannot build the foundations of its cathedrals on images, myths and legends, or even on dreams and poetry. This ground is not secure enough for it. It needs firmer facts. And where they do not exist, they have to be created.

The church has also done this. Already in the days of the old church fathers a process began in which the biblical images were transformed into biblical facts.

. . . and thus sense has degenerated into nonsense

People of antiquity and the Middle Ages were still hardly aware how incredible, even nonsensical and senseless, these images become if they are understood as actual events. After all, for them the whole of reality was still miraculous and the frontiers with unreality were fluid. What the church taught corresponded to their own thought.

However, since Galileo, Copernicus and Descartes at the beginning of modern times; at the latest since the Enlightenment, since Voltaire and Kant and the rise of the modern view of the world in the nineteenth and twentieth centuries; since Darwin and Einstein, it is no longer possible for enlightened men and women who think critically to accept these so-called 'facts' on which the church bases its faith without contradiction and scepticism.

Instead of giving insight into the truth of faith, the church's proclamation thus prevents people from grasping and accepting the 'truth' of which the Bible speaks. The result is not assent to the faith but at best courteous tolerance of those 'who still believe this kind of thing'.

Here is an example. As late as 1909 a Roman decision prescribed that the mythical-pictorial narrative about the creation of the woman from Adam's rib, which we find in the first chapter of the Bible, was to be believed as a historical fact. A profound account which figuratively emphasizes the unity and equality of man and woman became a factual absurdity, and the profound meaning of this account became sheer nonsense.

Statements which, understood as images, once made sense and illuminated the truth, often seem to present-day thinking to be sheer nonsense, in so far as they are meant to be believed in as factual accounts. They appear to be absurd claims which contradict all assured knowledge.

What are depicted in the church's preaching and teaching as historical facts are usually based on an interpretation of biblical texts which is simply wrong and does not do justice to the character of the Bible.

. . . which makes biblical faith ridiculous

When I first thumbed through the new Catechism, shortly after it was published in 1993, I could hardly believe my eyes when I still read in it that death made 'its entrance into human history' because 'our first parents were . . . tempted by the devil, disobeyed God's command' (cf. 1/ nos. 400, 390, 397). Certainly I had learned that as a child in religious instruction; but I did not know any of today's leading theologians who still interpreted the origin of death in this way.

The church's tradition refers to a sentence from Paul's letter to the Romans: 'Sin came into the world through one man and death through sin, and so death spread to all men because all men sinned' (Rom.5.12). Paul in turn owes this doctrine to the Jewish understanding of the mythical narrative of the fall of the first parents Adam and Eve in the first chapters of the Bible which was current in his time.

We find myths which interpret the origin of evil and death by a breach with the deity in many ancient religions. The myths gave people of that time an answer to their questions within such archaic pictures of the world. But if such myths are taught today as historical events, the imagery of the myths seems to most people to be absurd, indeed nonsensical. It comes to be misunderstood as a description of historical facts.

There has been death since the origin of life on earth; it is part of the process of living. Plants and animals have known death since life developed on this earth more than three billion years ago. In anthropogenetic terms these are our 'ancestors'. Only through the descent of our life from their life did 'death enter into human history', not from the disobedience of the 'first human beings'.

So wasn't it inevitable for me to doubt the teaching of a church which with an appeal to a 'divine revelation' still expects people to believe mythical images from long-past pictures of the world as a historical 'primeval event' (1/ no.390)? The pope still teaches that the well-known story from the Bible about the fall of Adam and Eve in paradise is an 'account' which despite its figurative language describes a 'primeval event' that took place 'at the beginning of the history of man'.

As a believing Catholic Christian must I really hold to be true what is taught by the supreme teaching authority of the church, namely, '. . . that the overwhelming misery which oppresses men and their inclination towards evil and death cannot be understood apart from their connection with Adam's sin' (1/ no.403). 'Revelation gives us the certainty of faith that the whole of human history is marked by the original fault freely committed by one of our parents' (1/ no.390).

What the supreme authority in the teaching office of the church expects present-day men and women to believe here as 'revealed truth' contradicts not only all assured scientific knowledge of modern times, but also the unanimous understanding of all biblical theologians who are to be taken seriously. If the pope today still describes this mythical biblical narrative as an 'account' of a historical 'primeval event', he is destroying the profound truth of this mythical narrative. Worse still, he is making biblical faith look ridiculous.

Written very angrily

After reading the account of the fall in the papal Catechism, as I wrote these 'notes', almost without noticing it, in my indignation I slipped into the style of a personal letter to the pope. I must get it off my chest.

Dear Pope,

I have just read in the Catechism for which you are responsible, and which you have commended, what you ask me and other believing Christians to believe as doctrine revealed by God about the fall of our first parents and the origin of evil and death. I had to read it twice because I did not think it possible that the church could still teach this sort of thing today.

However enlightened by the Holy Spirit you may be, while I am just a small lost sheep in your flock, here I cannot follow you. What you offer here as revealed truth seems to me to show contempt for anyone who seeks truth in the church's faith.

Now I have relied on the faith of the church, and all my life have tried not only to live it out but also to accept it intellectually and hand it on. I have not taken it lightly; I have taken it seriously. And then you come along and feed me like a stupid child with the absurd claim that 'the whole human race is marked by the primeval sin that our first parents willingly committed'.

Have you ever noted and taken in the way in which biblical criticism today explains the texts about paradise and the fall? Have you ever noted and taken in what the sciences have discovered about the development of the human race? How does your teaching about the entry of death into human history fit with present-day knowledge that only in the last millions of years have human beings developed from prior forms which we count as animals, and that people of the present species of *homo sapiens* came into being only around one hundred thousand years ago; that misery, pain and death had already accompanied life for many hundreds of millions of years previously, and therefore that human beings simply cannot have brought misery, evil, suffering and death into the world through a 'primeval sin' which they 'willingly committed'? All this was in the world long before there were human beings. Without death and the suffering bound up with it there would have been no higher development of life up to the human race. How does that square with your theology?

Have you never become aware how incredible it is to depict a biblical statement in the language of myth as a historical, factual 'primal event' in human history? If you go on forcing people to accept such ideas 'in the obedience of faith', you will drive more and more people from the church. Haven't you already turned your back on enough people since you became its leader?

When will you people up there in the highest offices of the

church understand that the church can no longer fob off people as it did in former centuries? The church is no longer facing uneducated and ignorant people who will accept from it anything that is presented to them as 'truth to be believed in', appealing to a divine revelation.

You have shut yourselves up in your old palace of apostolic tradition. You seek the truth only in the old chests that you keep in the cellar, or in the tomes that have been gathering dust in the attic for centuries. You are so certain that through the apostolic tradition you are in possession of infallible truth that you have become incapable of learning anything new. You offer people hungry for faith antiques instead of the truth.

Just open the windows of your fortress of faith. Not simply to elicit the homage of the crowd below. Look more closely at the people out there. They are not what you see from your perspective. With your thought and your arguments you are simply moving within your fortress. What you teach applies only within a closed system which is barricaded against the world, against thought, and against the thinking and the knowledge of present-day men and women.

If you only keep repeating the way in which people of antiquity and the Middle Ages understood and expressed their faith, you are not handing on the truth that they meant at that time. You will not fulfil your commission to communicate the message of Jesus to the world and to guard the apostolic tradition in this way. Liberate yourselves from your intellectual prison. Otherwise the faith of the church will degenerate into the teaching of a sect. Which is already largely what has happened!

Come out in front of your house once and for all, take a deep breath, and look around your buildings from outside, from a sufficient distance to give you a view of their surroundings as well. Then you will notice that you are living in a museum. Worse still, with your vestments, ceremonies and declarations you have become museum pieces. Can't you really see what impression you make on the people out there? At best, most people still gape at you as a curious piece of folklore in a museum. You can make an impression only on immature and ignorant masses. Other people feel repelled. At best they laugh tolerantly, as at a sectarian preacher.

Excuse me, dear Pope, for becoming so personal. But what you expect me to believe in your Catechism – and not just your teachings about the origin of misery and death – has really made me cross. Because it distorts the faith which I share with you and makes it incredible; because it prevents more and more thinking and informed people from assenting to this faith.

I'm afraid that you probably won't understand what makes me so angry. At best you will laugh tolerantly in an awareness of the superiority which your office gives you. Once again, please excuse me. And don't sent the police round straight away! For *lèse-majesté*!

Why does he keep quiet when he knows better?

I am not so certain whether the pope himself has sufficient knowledge of what the majority of his own theologians have recognized in questions relating to the historicity of the fall narrative. His thinking is stamped by the special situation of Polish Catholicism under the Communist regime. Polish theology was largely cut off from the theological development in the West and could only take part in its process of critical enlightenment to a limited degree. The inner consolidation of the church which was necessary for self-assertion and survival was more important for it than a critical enquiry into the biblical sources. I don't know to what degree the pope has considered how his doctrine of 'original sin' can be introduced into the context of the overall scientific investigation of the history of humankind.

But I can certainly assume that Cardinal Josef Ratzinger, who was a distinguished theologian before he rose to the highest hierarchies of the church, knows about the varied literary forms in which the Bible speaks. He might well know that the story of the fall is a myth which attempts to interpret the evil and suffering in the world that can be experienced today in terms of a breach between human beings and God caused by human guilt. This motif also appears in myths from other religions. No historical 'primeval event' is to be identified in the biblical account of the fall, not even 'in figurative language'. Ratzinger certainly knows that.

So why does he nevertheless present the myth of the fall as a historical fact? Against his better knowledge? I have only one explanation for this intellectual dishonesty: Ratzinger also knows that all the foundations would be swept away from the church and many of its doctrines should it prove that they are not based on the firm ground of reliably attested facts which have been 'handed down free of error'. And he's afraid of that. He conceals the truth from church people because he's afraid that the truth could damage the church.

Unless the fall were a historical fact, redemption would not be a historical fact either. And if that goes, then all the 'fruits of redemption' which have been entrusted to the church to administer and distribute also go down the river, along with the mitres and croziers of its supreme heads.

Images – not a depiction of historical events

Real events from the history of Israel and concrete historical experiences certainly underlie the biblical account, but the Bible does not interpret them in chronicles of events and accounts of fact but in the language of myth: in images and parables, in legends and sagas, in hymns and poems. Anyone who reads and understands these as depictions of historical events fails to understand what the Bible means to say.

Did God create the world in six days and rest on the seventh? No, he did not. No historical event is depicted here. What we have is the division into seven strophes of a hymn of praise which came into being in Jewish priestly circles during the Babylonian exile and is meant to be the basis for the sabbath commandment.

Were Adam and Eve the first human beings, who lived in paradise as the ancestors of our race? No, this is not a historical fact! There never has been a paradise, either on the planet earth or in the universe. Paradise is not a historical place in which the first human beings lived, but the hopeful image of a whole world in which human beings are in harmony with their origin, God, and therefore also live in harmony with themselves and the world. And Adam and Eve were not historically the first human beings. They never lived. They are simply an image for human beings.

Did God interrupt the building of the Tower of Babel by confusing people's languages out of anger at the evil of humankind? No, he did not. There are quite different reasons for the differences between languages. This narrative from the time of the Babylonian exile paints a picture which attempts to interpret human beings' inability to understand one another as a consequence of failing to be in harmony with God. Nor did the flood ever take place historically in the way depicted by the Bible. However, it might have its historical background in experiences of catastrophic inundations which often occurred in Mesopotamia between the Euphrates and the Tigris. The biblical account is a theological interpretation of such a natural catastrophe as 'God's punishment'.

Did the prophet Isaiah, enlightened by God, prophesy that a virgin would bear a child more than seven hundred years later? No, he did not. Centuries later the evangelist Matthew tore this passage from its original context and applied it to Jesus in order to depict him as the promised Messiah. It is an interpretation, not a fact.

Did Jesus make the 'blind see, the lame walk, lepers clean, the deaf hear, and the dead live again' (see Matt.11.5)? Jesus was probably active as a 'healer', like many others at that time, but such miracle stories are almost all figurative elaborations of Old

Testament messianic promises or transferences from Hellenistic myths.

Even the information that Jesus was thirty years old when he made his first public appearance, which seems so matter-of-fact, cannot be the basis for any inference about the chronology of his life. In Old Testament terminology the number thirty is to be regarded as a 'theological' number which denotes an ideal age. Moreover in the account of the Easter events, in which Jesus is said to have risen on the third day, the number 'three' has a symbolic theological and not a chronological significance.

Did Jesus deliver the great farewell discourses which are contained in John 14 to 17? No, the historical Jesus did not deliver any of these discourses. They are the result of reflection in the earliest Christian communities. They have been put into the mouth of Jesus so that he lends them his authority.

Did Pontius Pilate really say 'I find no fault in him' (Luke 23.4) when, as Luke reports, the Jews were calling for Jesus' death? No. This is not a historical fact but the expression of a bias, as when the Roman centurion under the cross exclaims, 'Truly, this was the Son of God' (Matt.27.54). The Christians could not proclaim to the Romans a Jesus whom they themselves had executed as a divine bringer of salvation. So the guilt for his death had to be shifted from the Romans to the Jews. This was an early cause of the later pogroms against the Jews.

Did Jesus at the Last Supper speak the words, 'This is my body which is given for you. This is my blood which is shed for you. Do this in memory of me', which interpret his death in advance, and thus institute the eucharist? No, he did not. These are not historical words of Jesus, but sayings which arose out of the cultic meals of the early Christians and which interpret the death of Jesus after the event as an atoning sacrifice. They are elements in a so-called cult legend.

This list of a few instances which spontaneously occur to me could be continued indefinitely. It would fill whole books. However, the result would always be the same: the 'object of faith' is not spectacular, miraculous historical events, but the truth which dawned on the people of the Bible in the events of the history of Israel and in their encounter with Jesus of Nazareth, a truth which the Bible depicts and preserves in the imagery of miracles, myths, sagas, legends, hymns of praise and visions.

But if I understand these images as a real depiction of miraculous historical events, I shut myself off from their truth. The encouragement to trust Jesus, who brings together God and human beings, degenerates into a demand to believe the most improbable and absurd miracles to be true. The credibility of the Bible is compromised.

Having to decide between unbelief and superstition

God, the great magician, who commands all the arts of miracle-working, no longer meets with admiration and applause. Rather, he comes up against suspicion and mistrust. He does not produce belief but unbelief.

Indeed, I regard the church's constant appeal to the miraculous intervention of an omnipotent God in the course of earthly history as one of the most important causes of the origin of modern atheism. Since the Enlightenment at least, educated and thinking people are no longer ready to be fobbed off with miracle stories by the church. Anyone who misunderstands myths and legends as accounts of historical events is forced into superstition. People look for faith, but the church's teaching all too often forces them to decide between superstition and unbelief.

Why does the church hierarchy, contrary to the better knowledge of the majority of its professional theologians, so stupidly insist on rooting the truth of faith in miraculous historical events? What is needed today is precisely the opposite.

In numerous conversations with people who were alienated from the faith of the church and the Bible or who even rejected it, and dismissed the church's doctrines as 'incredible nonsense',

I kept finding that something of the meaning and 'truth' of some church doctrines dawned on them when I explained to them that these accounts did not depict historical facts but were mythical images which had incorporated, worked over and pre-served deep existential human truths.

The historicization of myth by the church makes it more and more difficult for present-day people to assent to faith and forces them into unbelief.

9

The one on whom it depends

Jesus – Son of God?

On an adventurous drive right across Turkey, in the mosque of Edirne I made the acquaintance of a Muslim professor. He invited me to his home, hospitably gave me a meal, and even offered me a bed for the night. He told me that he was very fond of German classical music, especially Brahms, but didn't have much opportunity to hear this music in Turkey. I had some cassettes of classical music in my car, including Brahms. So after the meal we went out into the darkness, sat in the car, and together listened to Brahms' Violin Concerto. In that way we became friends.

Our conversation afterwards lasted deep into the night. Inevitably it was about Islam and Christianity, his faith and mine. He said that the worst thing about Christians was that they believed in three gods, the Father, the Son and the Holy Spirit. Islam was far superior to Christianity because it had preserved monotheism. That God, the one God, had a son who was born of an earthly woman seemed to him to be blasphemy. I attempted to correct his mistaken picture of Christian faith as well as my English allowed, by pointing out that in the Old Testament the title 'son of God' meant belonging to God, being accepted by God, indeed obedience to God, and had nothing to do with any association of God with a woman. But I couldn't convince him. The notion that God has a son born of an earthly woman seemed too unacceptable to him. Nor can believing Jews accept such an idea.

One could dismiss the view of this pious Muslim as a typical Islamic misunderstanding of Christian faith, were it not that Christian preaching, above all official church preaching, offers too many occasions for such a misapprehension.

Indeed, in the understanding of faith communicated by the church, the divine Sonship of Jesus is often seen in terms of biological procreation: Jesus is Son of God because he was not begotten by an earthly father but born from a virgin who 'conceived through the Holy Spirit'.

'Son of God' – a messianic title

The title 'Son of God' is itself much older than Christianity and was highly significant in the faith of Israel, in the Old Testament. There it has nothing to do with the descent of an eternal Son of God to earth and his incarnation by divine pro-creation in the womb of a virgin.

According to ideas influential at that time, a child first became a 'son' when his father picked him up and thus recognized him, accepted him and confirmed him as his son. The title 'son' expressed election, care, recognition, acceptance, confirmation, elevation, and also authorization to act 'in the name of the father'. The son is subordinate to his father and obedient to him.

In this sense the whole people of Israel was called 'son of God'. David, the king of Israel, was also called 'son of God', though no one doubted that he had been fathered by a man and born of a woman. The kings of Israel also bore this title. The Bible uses it to indicate that they were under God, that they did not rule in their own power but on the basis of an election by God. Only if they maintained this obedience towards God would their rule become a blessing and salvation for the people. Only where the will of Yahweh was done, i.e. where God 'ruled' in the people, did salvation come about. And if the king turned away from God and no longer obeyed him, but grounded his power in himself, disaster came. At any rate, that is what the prophets kept saying.

In Judaism, these notions later gave rise to the image of a Messiah sent by God who had been chosen by God and was utterly obedient to him. This Messiah would restore the rule of God in Israel. He was called 'the Lord's anointed', like the kings of Israel after they had been anointed. The word 'Messiah' means the anointed – Christ in Greek.

The Messiah, the Christ, was a 'son of God' like King David. The designation 'son of God' is a title for the hoped-for redeemer, the Christ. The name does not mean that the Messiah himself is 'divine' or even a god. Like David of old, the Messiah was regarded as a man chosen by God to fulfil the will of God and thus bring salvation: a new David, a branch of David. 'Son of God' was in practice another name for Messiah or Christ.

One of us

When Jesus' disciples and his Jewish followers called him 'son of God', they were simply expressing their belief that Jesus of Nazareth was the hoped-for Messiah, the redeemer of Israel sent by God. They certainly did not think that Jesus was a divine person who lived as a human being among them.

They certainly did not see the man with whom they went round the country; with whom they spoke, ate, drank and slept; as a God who been in God as 'Son' from before the beginning of time and now had been born of a virgin. That would have offended their strict Jewish monotheism as much as it offended my Muslim professor in Edirne.

Even when the Jews in Jerusalem were arguing whether Jesus was the son of God or not, they were not arguing about whether he was a God or 'only a human being'; they were arguing about whether he was the Messiah. It would not have occurred to any of them to see in Jesus, the carpenter's son, a god descended to earth.

Jesus' family knew nothing of his divinity. Mary completely failed to understand her son, despite the instruction given to her by an angel, as depicted by Luke. And his kinsfolk simply thought him crazy (Mark 3.21). It is also striking that at no point in the Gospels does Jesus appeal to his being begotten by the Holy Spirit and mention his birth from a virgin mother.

Although the Gospels later paint over the human figure of Jesus to make him divine, it is clear from many passages from the earliest narrative traditions of the New Testament that the historical Jesus, too, did not see himself as a divine person. Nor did he think that he was morally perfect. When someone called him 'Good master', he retorted, 'Only one is good', namely God (Matt.19.17).

I see Jesus primarily as a human being. For me he is even the normative human being. As a human being he was born from a quite normal human woman. Nor do the narratives of his birth from a virgin compel us to assume that the human being Jesus of Nazareth was fathered and born in a different way from other human beings. As a human being he lived, taught, believed, hoped and suffered. And as a human being he died. One of us!

Was he married?

We do not know whether Jesus was married. We shall probably never know. But we cannot completely rule out the possibility, although there is no mention of it in the Gospels. The Jewish scholar Schalom Ben Chorim, who is to be taken seriously, gives good reasons for supposing that Jesus was married:

'My view is that Jesus of Nazareth was married, like any rabbi in Israel. His disciples and his opponents would have questioned him had he departed from this universal custom . . . Now people will say that we do not read a single word about a wife or children of Jesus. That is true, but we don't

read a word about the disciples' wives either. Were they all
unmarried, quite contrary to the Jewish custom of this time
and all times?'

An unmarried rabbi would not have been taken seriously
(19/104f.).

The Christian tradition felt that a possible link between Jesus
and a woman was in conflict with his divine sonship and therefore excluded it, just as it turned the 'brothers and sisters of
Jesus' into kinsfolk. I would have no difficulties here. The meaning that Jesus has for me would not change. Nor do I see it as a
contradiction to his divinity. If God, as the church teaches,
became fully man in Jesus and 'has become like to us in all
things, except sin' (Heb.4.15), the love of the young man Jesus
for a woman is no less part of his full and true humanity than
eating, drinking, sleeping, speaking, feeling and breathing.

Unless one saw love between man and woman, unlike eating,
feeling and breathing, as contrary to God, as sin!

Omniscient?

Was Jesus omniscient? I have my doubts. He only became
omniscient later, when he had been elevated to the status of a
divine being. As a child the human Jesus probably had to learn
to read and probably also to write, just like any other children.
What he did not know, he had to ask about, like any other
human being. How much bread do you have? What is your
name? How long has he had this disease? However, the papal
Catechism also has an answer for this normal human
behaviour: 'He would even have to inquire for himself about
what one in the human condition can learn only from experience. This corresponded to the reality of his voluntary emptying
of himself, "taking the form of a slave"' (1/ no.472).

I believe that Jesus' view of the world corresponded to the
knowledge of his time and the ideas of his environment. He

shared with his contemporaries notions of the activity of spirits and demons, angels and the devil. Some scholars conjecture that Jesus was influenced by Hellenistic schools of philosophy active in Galilee. Near Nazareth, in Gadara, there was a Cynic settlement. Its itinerant preachers went through places in Galilee and proclaimed their teaching. Some elements of Jesus' teaching show such striking parallels to the teachings of these philosophers that we cannot exclude the possibility that Jesus took it over from them.

Jesus certainly did not know that the earth is only a planet orbiting the sun, nor did he know that the continent of America lay still undiscovered across the Atlantic. Nor could he have understood Chinese. And he would have had no inkling that two thousand years later a pope would be residing in Rome who called himself his authorized representative.

The account of the twelve-year-old Jesus amazing the scholars in the temple with his wisdom because of his divine knowledge is not historical; it is a later legend which is meant to illustrate the divine origin of Jesus.

Had a sage theologian talked with Jesus about the most holy Trinity, Jesus would probably have looked at him uncomprehendingly. He drew his religious knowledge from the Jewish tradition which was taught in the synagogue. In essentials his teaching was modelled on Jewish faith, though it assumed its quite special emphasis and decisiveness only on the lips of Jesus. Neither the teaching that human beings are children of God nor the command to love one's neighbour are new. The Old Testament also already speaks of loving one's enemy.

In his message about the dawn of the rule of God, the centre of his historical preaching, Jesus takes up statements about the Jewish expectation of the end-time. Like Jewish eschatology, Jesus too announces that the coming of the new world will be preceded by a collapse of the old. Then 'the sun will darken and the moon will no longer give her light'. 'The stars will fall from heaven' (cf. Mark 13.19 with Isa.13.10; 34.4).

Even if the sayings of this 'end-time discourse' had already

been prefigured in Judaism or the discourse was composed later
by Jewish-Christian communities from Old Testament sayings,
and the historical Jesus did not formulate it and utter it himself,
we may assume that he thought and talked like this. These sayings correspond both to his religious views and to his view of
the world. Like his contemporaries, he too naively imagined
that on the coming of God the stars would fall to earth from
heaven, because this was written in Isaiah the prophet.
Although according to Colossians 'everything in the world,
heaven and earth, were made by him' (1.16), Jesus had no
better knowledge of the cosmology of the universe than other
people of his time.

Inerrant?

Nor was Jesus inerrant. He was wrong even in a quite decisive
point of his message: he proclaimed that the coming of the kingdom of God in Israel was imminent: 'Truly, this generation will
not pass away until all this takes place' (Mark 13.30). 'There
are some of you who will not taste of death until they see the
kingdom of God coming in power' (Mark 9.1). So Jesus
believed that the end of the world would already take place during the lifetime of his contemporaries, and then everything,
including human beings, would be transformed and recreated.

We now know that Jesus' expectation of an imminent end
was wrong. Nothing changed in the world; it did not perish, nor
has it been transformed. The earliest church already had to
postpone its expectation of the dawn of the rule of God further
and further, although I Peter continued to comfort those who
hoped: 'The end of all things is at hand.' The failure of the
arrival of the kingdom of God, in which everything would turn
to good, still caused the earliest church many headaches, until it
finally solved the problem by teaching that the kingdom of God
had already dawned, but was still 'hidden'. However, one day it
would be 'consummated' in eternal life. Then 'God will wipe

away all tears. Death will be no more. Nor will there be mourning, lamentation and tribulation'.

Jesus the Jew

During a visit to Vienna I allowed friends to persuade me to go with them to Grinzing to sample the new wine. It didn't give me a hangover!

An older man was sitting opposite me at the long narrow wooden table in the vintner's courtyard. His clothing and beard suggested that he was an Orthodox Jew. I got into conversation with him. He had lost his family in the concentration camps and had himself escaped the bloody Holocaust only by chance. 'The Christians have always persecuted the Jews,' he said. I couldn't contradict this historical fact, but emphasized that as a Christian I couldn't understand this behaviour on the part of Christians, since Jesus, whom they confess as Son of God, had himself been a Jew. That should have led to friendship and solidarity with the Jews. In the midst of the loud celebrations, warmed by the wine, our conversation unexpectedly took on depth and earnestness.

'As a Jew, what do you really think of Jesus?,' I asked him. 'Who was Jesus?' He had a sip of wine and then explained to me: 'Jesus was a reformer of the Jewish religion, like your Jan Hus or Martin Luther. He clashed with the priesthood like all prophets. So he had to die.' That's a brief summary of what he took much longer to say.

At that time his interpretation of Jesus was a new one for me. Jesus, a failed reformer of the Jewish religion? I had never looked at it like that before. At that time I couldn't accept this view, because it didn't seem enough to me. But it impressed me and stuck in my memory. Nowadays I am more inclined to accept its probability, especially since reading books by Ben-Chorin and Pinchas Lapide.

When we begin to see Jesus' words and actions as the words

and actions of one Jew among others and understand his words against the background of Jewish thought, his message takes on a surprising new meaning and is more illuminating than in the accustomed patterns of thought of the Greek and Latin understanding of him.

The picture of Jesus in the church and Christianity has in fact failed to pay sufficient attention to Jesus' roots in Jewish piety, Jewish thought and Jewish faith. The deductive theology of the Logos made flesh, derived from Greek thought, has degraded the Jewish people so that they are simply the landing ground of the Son of God descending from heaven. This makes the figure of the Son of God strangely colourless, bloodless and abstract, despite his divine splendour.

Jesus the prophet

The figure of Jesus cannot be detached from his Jewish origin, his Jewish environment and his Jewish religion. The question who Jesus was and what he wanted can only be answered within this context.

Jesus was a believing Jew. He was not a priest nor a monk. He was a quite ordinary 'layman'. He held no office in the church; he was no organization man. Nor was he a trained theologian, a scribe. He did not guard any 'sacred traditions', nor was his activity that of studying the Law.

He can best be described with a word which he also applied to himself: he was a prophet. And that is what the people of the time also said of him: he was one of the prophets. 'He was a prophet, mighty in deed and word before God and all the people' (Mark 8.28).

Israel's religion had kept producing prophets, men who at particular historical moments emerged with the claim to be advocating God's cause. They did not proclaim any doctrines, any infallible truths; they spoke directly to the situation of the people. They spoke to people's consciences, aroused them, threatened them, intervened, called for a change in thought and circumstances. They gave courage, they comforted, they offered visions of a better future, they opened up new ways. They did not stand on the side of the established orders. Rather, they caused unrest and were usually opposed by the guardians of the temple and the palace. In their voices Israel heard the claim, promise and instructions of the God who had once brought the people out of slavery in Egypt. The prophets spoke and acted in the spirit of God.

If the person of Jesus in its uniqueness can be assigned to any group, then it can most easily be assigned to that of the prophets of Israel. Jesus, too, is someone who, 'seized with the spirit of God', came forward with the claim to be proclaiming God's will and speaking in God's name. He gave people the courage to entrust their lives to God. And in the face of the ritualized temple God of the priests, the domesticated bookish God of the scribes, and the pedantic God of order taught by the casuistic teachers of the Law, he re-established the living, personal God from the early days of Israel. His God is the same God of whom the great prophets of Israel had also spoken. So he too drew down upon himself the deadly enmity of the priestly religious bureaucrats who finally also brought him to the cross.

Jesus sharply criticized the powerful, castigated the exploitation of the poor, and attacked social abuses. Such circumstances did not correspond to the will of God. God wants freedom. God wants mercy. So although Jesus was not a politician or the leader of a political liberation movement, he also aroused the suspicions of the state power. Although he kept away from the rebellious anti-Roman movements in his country, renounced the sword and called for non-violence, he was nevertheless executed by the Roman state authorities as a political rebel. The fate of a prophet!

Jesus the Son of God

The transformation of the Jewish Messiah Jesus into an eternal godlike Son of God who descended from heaven began only a few years after his crucifixion.

The belief of the earliest Jewish community in the messiahship of Jesus was also adopted by Jews who lived outside Judaea in Hellenistic culture; they spoke Greek and thought in Greek. And through these people the message of Jesus, the Messiah, also reached the other peoples in the Hellenistic environment of Judaism, the so-called 'Gentiles'. When these non-Jews heard of a son of God called Jesus they did not associate the notion of the Jewish messianic expectation with this. That was really important only for people who had grown up in the Jewish tradition of thought. It was alien to non-Jews and must have seemed to them to be a domestic Jewish matter. They heard talk of Jesus the Son of God with other ears, Hellenistic ears. They too were very familiar with the notion of a Son of God, and for them it was highly significant. For them, too, the name 'Son of God' did not necessarily denote a divine being. Usually important and prominent people were honoured with this title.

The Egyptian Pharaoh was regarded as a son of God. The Roman emperors became gods after their death. Augustus was revered as a god even during his lifetime. In the myths, Heracles and Dionysus were sons of a god. They had emerged from the union of Zeus with an earthly woman. Even historical figures like Homer, Pythagoras, Plato, Alexander the Great and Pompey were called 'son of god'. The boundaries between 'divine' and 'human' were still fluid at that time. There was nothing unusual in a person saying that he was a son of god.

I can well imagine that for people in the Hellenistic cultural circles in which Christianity came into being it was not difficult also to say the same thing of Jesus. Perhaps this title, which was familiar to them, even helped them to emphasize and express the meaning of Jesus. However, they associated different ideas with the name 'Son of God' from those of the Jewish biblical tradition. Their notions of a son of God were mixed up with Jewish ideas, and thus the original meaning of this title also changed.

With this transformation, notions from Hellenistic mythology, the emperor cult and Greek philosophy also entered the picture which the New Testament paints of Jesus, the crucified one. In the mission to the Gentiles carried on by the earliest church the Jewish Messiah, the obedient servant of God, became a Greek Christ with a divine aura. The Jewish messianic title 'son of God' came to denote a Son of God equal to God in the metaphysical sense. The man Jesus, who was obedient to God, himself became a God 'who rules for ever'.

And the Jewish renewal movement became a world religion: Christianity. The kingdom of God which had been announced became the rule of the church.

The 'Christ of faith'

The transformation of the image of Jesus from that of a Jewish Messiah into that of a divine bringer of salvation for the whole world is above all the work of Paul, a highly educated Jew who came from Tarsus, a Hellenistic city in the south of present-day Turkey. Many scholars of religion say that he, and not Jesus, is the real founder of Christianity. Without Paul, Jesus' cause would have remained a domestic Jewish affair. Perhaps a Jewish sect bearing the name Jesus might have come into being, but not Christianity.

It is not certain whether Paul ever knew Jesus personally. It is striking that in all his writings Paul reports virtually nothing about the life and activity of Jesus. He does not provide any biographical details about Jesus in them. The historical Jesus is completely overlaid by the figure of the divine Christ. What the real Jesus did and said does not even seem to interest him. I have read that he mentions the name of Jesus only fifteen times in his writings, as opposed to the name Christ, which he uses three hundred and seventy-eight times. Paul does not hand on any words from the mouth of Jesus. He does not report any of his actions. He does not proclaim the teaching of Jesus; he proclaims his own teaching. The source on which he draws is not Jesus, but an 'illumination' by the 'spirit'.

Paul created a completely new figure, the 'Christ of faith'. And this figure no longer bears much resemblance to the real Jesus. Whereas the image of the historical Jesus increasingly disappears into the background, the image of the exalted Christ is elaborated in more and more forms, enriched with more and more detail, and heightened so that it becomes divine. A godlike figure arose on to which all perfections and all powers were projected.

The cross, which sealed Jesus' failure as Messiah, became the sign of victory. And the battered man who had hung on it became the Son of God who had come down to offer himself as an atoning sacrifice and who through this rose to be the redeemer of all humankind.

This Christ was there 'before ever the world was made'. 'All things were created through him and for him' (Col.1.15-17). The carpenter's son from Nazareth became the creator of the cosmos and the divine ruler of the worlds. 'He is the reflection of the glory of God and an image of his being,' writes the Letter to the Hebrews, and the Letter to the Philippians goes even further, by speaking of an 'equality with God'.

The church could time and again appeal irrefutably to this figure of Christ and justify its own authority by him in a way which it could not with the historical person Jesus. So even today in the church, in the liturgy, in sermons and in the Catechism, there is far more talk of Christ than there is of Jesus.

The Gospels

Paul had related virtually nothing of the life and activity of Jesus. That does not seem to have interested him. Probably, too, he had hardly any specific information about Jesus' life. He proclaimed only one thing: the Crucified One is the Christ.

However, most believers think that we come upon the real Jesus in the four Gospels. They hope that there they can experience who Jesus really was, where he was born, where he lived, what he did and said. There they hope to discover facts which give them a reliable picture of the real Jesus.

Most ordinary believers cannot make much of the letters of Paul from which extracts are read aloud to them in worship. By contrast, the Gospels, which came into being later, with their vivid narratives, seem finally to give them what they want. The Gospels grip not only the mind, but also the heart and the imagination.

However, anyone in search of the historical truth about Jesus and his activity is not much better served by the Gospels than by the letters of Paul. Here too the real Jesus is almost completely overlaid by the figure of the exalted Christ of faith.

Although there are also many biographical details from the life of Jesus and contemporary events in the four Gospels, it is not their purpose to provide a biography of Jesus. In the last resort they do not set out to relate facts from his life and document his discourses word for word. They want what Paul also wanted: to proclaim faith in the crucified Messiah whom God 'has exalted to be Lord'. However, they do this with other means, through narrative description.

They see the person, the words and actions, the life and death of Jesus, in the light of the Easter faith. The figure of the historical Jesus of Nazareth is theologically overpainted by the post-Easter faith and disappears almost completely behind the towering pictures which the authors of the Gospels paint of the 'Christ of faith'. Where the description of concrete events, with precise details about place, time and persons, gives the impression of being an account of events which actually took place, in reality we usually have artistic theological constructions.

No description of the life of Jesus

We know only a little about the real Jesus who lived and worked at that time in the land of the Jews. Only laborious scholarly work can filter out from the Gospels references to the words, life and actions of the historical person Jesus.

Only part of what the Jesus of the Gospels taught and preached belongs to the *ipsissima verba* of Jesus, i.e. the words which the historical Jesus himself spoke in this form. Most of his sayings, teachings and discourses in the Gospels are 'community formations'; in other words, they were formulated for the first time in the post-Easter communities, in their life, their worship and their preaching. These words mostly derived from the meditations of believers on Jesus, theological reflection, or came into being out of the need for clarification in concrete discussions in the earliest church. So they give us only indirect information about who Jesus really was and what he really taught; rather, they give us information about what was believed about him in the communities. They are interpretations of Jesus against the background of the Jewish faith and Hellenistic ideas.

For example, we cannot be certain about where Jesus was born. Bethlehem, where Luke makes the miraculous birth take place, is a result of Luke's theological concern to emphasize Jesus as the promised Messiah, the 'shoot of David'; for David came from Bethlehem. The birth in Bethlehem is a theological statement, not a biographical one.

The answer to the question whether Jesus did miracles depends on what we understand by miracle. However, miracles can hardly be regarded as historical facts. Most miracle stories in the New Testament are attempts to depict the significance of Jesus by transforming Old Testament passages into narratives. They depict Jesus as the one from whom the prophets hoped for the deliverance of Israel. Biblical critics have recognized in some miracle stories a transference of motifs from Hellenistic accounts of the deeds of ancient heroes and gods, the veneration of whom in the period of the earliest church competed with the veneration of Jesus.

Even the passion narratives in the four Gospels are conceived through and through in theological terms, though with different emphases. For example, they interpret the fate of Jesus under the Old Testament image of the suffering servant of God, who as the 'lamb of God' does atonement through his suffering and death for the sins of the many and through his blood establishes a new covenant between Israel and its God. They depict the story of the passion on the basis of models which are many hundreds of years older and cannot be regarded as a reliable source for the actual course of the passion of Jesus.

These few examples, which occur to me spontaneously, are enough to keep me aware of what biblical criticism has been able to demonstrate in countless other examples: the historical Jesus indeed underlies the image that the Gospels paint of Jesus, and biographical details from his life and activity also flicker through, but the overall portrait is not a direct description of the life and actions of the historical Jesus of Nazareth.

The New Testament is not concerned to hand on historical facts; it is concerned to propagate the belief that Jesus is the Christ.

What we find in the Gospels are myths, legends, sagas, images, parables, invented speeches, scriptural proofs turned into narratives, miracle stories, visions, hymns, etc., but no reliable information about the real Jesus and his activity. At best we can get to know the historical echo to Jesus' activity from the New Testament.

This knowledge of the theologians seldom gets out of the lecture rooms of the universities to people through the pulpits. Why should the faithful be disturbed?

Increasingly overlaid by the divine Christ

We can see clearly in the four Gospels how with the increasing
chronological distance from Jesus' death his figure is depicted in
an increasingly godlike way and his divinity is increasingly
heightened. The carpenter's son from Nazareth increasingly
becomes a Son of God.

The Gospel of Mark is the oldest of the four Gospels, and thus
closest in time to the historical Jesus. Scholars tell us that it was
composed between around AD 67 and 70, i.e. around thirty-five
years after the death of Jesus. The Gospels of Matthew and Luke
were composed some years later. Both took up and altered narrative material from the Gospel of Mark and in addition also
drew on their own sources. The Gospel of John, which differs
considerably from the first three Gospels in style and content,
may have been written around a century after the birth of Jesus.

In Mark, Jesus is first proclaimed Son of God at his baptism
in the Jordan by a voice from the clouds. In Matthew and Luke
the child in his mother's womb is already God's Son. In the
manger he is surrounded with divine splendour. And in John,
Jesus is proclaimed as the pre-existent Logos who was for eternity with God even before his birth. 'In the beginning was the
Word. And the Word was God. All things were made by him.'

In the Gospel of Mark, the oldest, the figure of the human
Jesus is still depicted clearly in the background of the portrait
of Jesus. Here Jesus still speaks like a human being. He tells
stories, he asks questions, he listens, he argues, he meets people,
he disputes. In John he delivers long and ceremonial speeches
like a divine teacher from a lofty throne, in poetic language
which was really comprehensible only to those with a philo-
sophical training.

Jesus' power to perform miracles is also heightened. Jairus's
little daughter, whom Jesus delivers from death in Mark, is 'only
sleeping'. The young man of Nain, of whom only Luke tells us,
is lying on his bier and is being buried when Jesus awakens
him. John heightens the miracle further: Lazarus has been lying

in the tomb for four days and is 'already stinking' when Jesus calls him back to life (Mark 5.39; Luke 7.11; John 11.39).

In Mark, when Jesus dies, 'the curtain of the temple is rent in two from top to bottom'. In Matthew, nature plays a more vigorous part in the death of its co-creator: 'The earth quaked, the rocks split, and the graves opened.'

In Mark and Matthew Jesus dies on the cross with the cry of the godforsaken man in Psalm 22, 'My God, my God, why have you forsaken me?' The idea of a Messiah forsaken by God is already intolerable for Luke. He beautifies the scene and brings harmony to it with a saying from Psalm 31, 'Father, into your hands I commend my spirit.' Jesus does not die making a desperate accusation against his God; he places himself as trustingly as a child in his Father's hands. It is quite different later in John. Here Jesus makes no complaint; here he has become a victor, sovereign in his accomplishment. He says only, 'It is accomplished.'

A mere seventy years after his death, the figure of the human Jesus had been almost completely overlaid by the figure of the divine Christ. Of course the official church also knows about these differences in the account of the four Gospels. But it has another explanation of them: through the activity of the Holy Spirit, the knowledge of Christ has kept progressing in the church.

The picture of Jesus – painted from Old Testament models

The Gospels are an account of early Christian preaching. In so far as the preaching of Jesus was addressed to the Jews, the early Christians, who were themselves also Jews, referred back to the Holy Scriptures in order to prove with their help that Jesus was the promised Messiah, the new David, the new Moses. Individual sentences or images from the writings of the prophets were transformed into stories about Jesus.

For example, the flight into Egypt and the massacre of the infants in Bethlehem in Mark's infancy narrative were not meant to depict historical events from the childhood of Jesus. Rather, with the help of quotations from the Old Testament and by association with themes from the childhood of Moses, they were meant to convince Jewish listeners that Jesus was the Messiah. In many stories of miracles which Jesus performed, like the healings of the blind, the deaf and the paralysed, the stilling of the storm and the multiplication of loaves, motifs from the Old Testament were transferred to Jesus. The song of praise which Mary utters after her visit to Elizabeth, the Magnificat, is composed almost exclusively of fragments from the Old Testament. Jewish Christians in the early church who were expert in scripture built the stones into an artistic theological structure.

New Testament scholars can demonstrate how the account of the life of Jesus in the Gospels has been shaped chapter by chapter, text by text, almost sentence by sentence, by Old Testament models. Even the passion narratives, which seem to us to be so documentary, have been artistically constructed down to the smallest details according to plans and with material drawn from the Jewish Bible. They give us little information about what really happened.

Transferences from pagan myths?

When the Christian faith extended into the world of 'pagan' Hellenism, ideas from other religions and myths of antiquity were also taken over and put at the service of the preaching of Christ. In this way these ideas and myths also found their way into the descriptions in the Gospels. We must reckon that much that the Gospels relate about Jesus was once related in a similar form about Hellenistic heroes and deities and transferred to Jesus.

For example, the striking similarity between Christian

doctrine and the doctrine of the cult of Mithras is well known. The religion of Mithras had found its way into the Roman empire from Persia at around the same time as early Christianity, and competed with it. Mithras, too, had come down from heaven. Shepherds worshipped him at his birth. He did much good in his earthly life and held a farewell meal with his followers before he returned to heaven. The words 'Do this in remembrance of me. This is my body, this is my blood' are also said to have been spoken at the cultic meals of followers of Mithras (cf. 17/ 337). Mithras was exalted into heaven by the sun god and shared in his omnipotence. He was called 'mediator between God and man' and became a saviour and redeemer. Can these parallels really only be chance ones?

The birthday of Mithras was celebrated in Rome on 25 December. In 353 the church fixed the birthday of Jesus on this day. The church's symbols of Peter the rock, the cock and the keys are also said originally to have been symbols of the sun god Mithras. And the mitres with which the heads of the Catholic hierarchy are adorned come from the priests of Mithras.

So what do I think when I note the following information from comparative religion?

Like Jesus, Pythagoras, the great philosopher and mathematician of the sixth century BC, began his teaching activity with a miracle involving fishes. It is said that he taught the people in images and parables, healed the sick, and even stilled a storm on the sea. He was mocked and persecuted. He descended into hell and rose from the dead. He was regarded as a son of the god Apollo.

It is said that on the death of Caesar the sun was darkened, darkness set in, the earth quaked and the dead rose.

Even in the time of Jesus Heracles was revered as saviour, son of God and mediator. Like the Johannine Jesus he died with the words 'It is accomplished'. The Babylonian Marduk, sent by his father to earth as redeemer, was 'captured, interrogated, condemned to death, scourged and executed with a criminal'.

There are also precursors to many miracles of Jesus in the

pagan myths. Like Jesus, Asclepius from Epidaurus, the god of healing, was depicted as a physician and saviour. Like Jesus, he healed the dumb and the paralysed; like Jesus, he called for faith. He stilled storms and raised the dead (cf. 7/83ff., 90, 92).

Comparative religion has collected a wealth of such similarities to pre-Christian myths in the depiction of Jesus in the Gospels. We cannot simply ignore them. I would not venture to judge whether and to what degree they have been deliberately transferred to Jesus. At all events, there is a suspicion that they had at least an indirect effect on the formation of the picture of Jesus, because they were a quite normal and natural element of the religious thought and language of the time in which the Gospels were written.

Imperial purple for the carpenter's son

In Luke's account of the birth of Jesus, an angel appears to the shepherds in the fields, and proclaims to them who the newborn child in the manger is: 'I bring you good news. To you is born in the city of David a saviour, who is Messiah and Lord.' Here Luke has put into the mouth of the angel a title of Jesus by which the early church expressed the significance that Jesus had acquired for it since his death.

In the New Testament Jesus is called not only Son of God and Messiah (= Christ) but also Lord, Redeemer, Saviour and Liberator. These titles derive both from the terminology of the Old Testament and also from the ideas of the pagan environment. They were transferred to Jesus.

The translators of the Old Testament had already used the originally oriental title 'Lord' (Greek Kyrios), which was given to rulers, to render the Hebrew name of God, Yahweh. The Jews say 'the Lord' when they speak of God. They also praise their God as redeemer, liberator and bringer of salvation.

The title Kyrios was applied to the emperor by the Romans. In Christian worship the praise of the emperor still echoes in the

Kyrie of the mass: 'Kyrie eleison, Lord have mercy.' Similarly, the emperors bore the title liberator, saviour (*soter*) and even saviour of the world.

The expression 'good news' (= *euangelion* – *evangelium*) used by the angel to proclaim the advent of the Messiah also derives from the imperial cult and was used to proclaim that a new ruler had ascended the throne.

The man from Nazareth was not only dressed in the concealing garments of the biblical God in order to emphasize that he was Messiah and Son of God; the Christ was also decked in imperial robes of purple.

From whom does salvation come?

About a century ago, a Roman inscription was found in the Turkish city of Priene. It dates from the year 9 BC and proclaims that the birthday of the emperor is to be celebrated as a festival throughout the world. Years ago I included the text of this inscription in a school book about the Christmas texts. The pupils were meant to recognize from a comparison with the biblical texts that the biblical message of Christmas did not depict some tranquil idyll but is explosive and provocative, with political and social connotations.

The inscription runs,

'This day, the birthday of the emperor, has given the whole world a different appearance. It would have perished had not a common good fortune shone out for all men and women in the one who is born today. Those who judge rightly will see this birthday as the beginning of life for themselves. Providence has filled this man with gifts for the salvation of mankind and sent him to us as saviour. He will put an end to all war and bring splendour everywhere. Through his appearance the hopes of our ancestors are fulfilled. It is impossible that anyone greater should come. The birthday of this god is the beginning of all good news for the world.'

Anyone who has any ear at all for the linguistic formulae of the Bible and the Christian way of speaking about the significance of the birth of Jesus will immediately note in perplexity that almost the same words and images are used here as in connection with the birth of Jesus. What is stated by the imperial Roman cult about Augustus is said in the New Testament, with a provocative change, of Jesus Christ: salvation and peace in the world do not come from the brilliant and powerful emperor, but from the helpless child who is lying peacefully in the manger. Salvation is not expected of political, economic and military powers, but of someone who has no power, but was deeply rooted in God and therefore was one who loved, forgave and served.

At that time I wrote for the pupils:

'The more we entrust our life to the one whom the Christmas stories proclaim as Messiah, the more we can succeed in achieving a life in which salvation, i.e. love and friendship, truth and trust, a life with human dignity and shared good fortune, become more important than the pursuit of money and wealth, power and status, satisfaction and consumption. To take the way of Jesus is to grasp a realistic opportunity that things will become somewhat better in our own lives, and also in the world.'

That is what I wrote then. And I have no reason to take back a word of it now.

Which Jesus?

It was the figure of *Jesus* which in my youth led me to make a decision for the Christian faith. He was the one who convinced me. He was the one to whom I attached myself. In the teaching of Jesus I found a truth which I could adopt for myself. Through him, too, I again came into contact with a 'reality' which plays the decisive role in the life of Jesus. And because I believed in him, because I found truth in him, because he came to show me the way, I also found my way into the church, almost as a second step. Most people usually do things the other way round.

Now, after the event, as a result of my reflections in these 'notes', I have become more strongly aware than before how much the figure of the historical Jesus has been painted over by the divinized picture of the post-Easter Christ So I keep thinking, 'Which Jesus impressed me so much at that time, shaped me, drew me to him? Was it the man from Nazareth or was it perhaps the "Christ of faith"?'

I must confess that at that time I had no idea that these two figures could be distinguished. At that time my picture of Jesus was still essentially influenced by the picture painted by Romano Guardini in his book *The Lord*. The historical Jesus was as the Gospels described him to me: a man full of love and goodness, truth and wisdom; full of the power to perform miracles, speaking and acting with divine authority. I saw him as one who was there to help, heal, forgive, raise up men and women; who was free from all evil and wickedness, free from error and free from sin. He was of divine origin and lived wholly in harmony with God, even to death.

One could certainly attach oneself to such a person. I need not excuse myself for that today.

Only a typical adolescent process?

Psychologically – as I now recognize quite clearly – it was the ideal figure of Jesus who had captivated me: the 'Christ of faith' who in a steady development in the Gospels had been elevated so that he became an increasingly perfect and divine figure.

Only now, after the event, can I recognize with the help of psychology that I went through a process of being shaped by an ideal image, which is typical of adolescence. As Konrad Lorenz has pointed out, at a personal and a human level this process resembles the process by which young animals are moulded to follow their parents.

So was it only by this kind of psychological process that I began to believe in Jesus Christ? This suspicion, which comes to me as I write, confuses me. The notion that it could have been 'just this' and not 'much more' which led me to believe upsets the understanding of my faith that I have had so far.

Hitherto I had always thought that I came to believe because I was 'touched' by God in an encounter with Jesus. And now? Is it nothing but an ordinary everyday process of being moulded by an ideal figure in my youth?

A sobering thought.

The loser and the winner

In my encounter with the Jesus of the Gospels, without knowing it I came upon an exaggerated picture of the human being Jesus of Nazareth which divinized him. The splendour of this picture gripped me.

Have human beings shaped this divinized picture of Jesus in order to create for themselves a perfect figure to which they can hold fast? Or is church tradition right? According to tradition, people illuminated by the spirit of God recognized increasingly clearly after Easter who the controversial rabbi from Galilee, who had ended as a rebel on the cross, really was, namely the incarnate Son of God.

Is the 'Christ' of the Gospels the result of a human quest, prompted by need, for an exalted leader to guarantee them guidance, support and hope? Could it be that the earlier followers of Jesus, disappointed by the real Jesus who had not achieved what was hoped of him, created a new 'bearer of hope', the 'Christ of faith'?

This Christ was no loser, like the man on the cross. From the beginning he was a winner! One is better off with winners, and legends are always more beautiful than reality.

Born in the human heart?

Jesus of Nazareth was 'born of woman'. He was a man with blood in his veins. The 'Christ of faith' was born in human hearts and heads.

The basic material of his figure, like clay, derives from memories of the historical Jesus. Images and figures from the Old Testament and the Hellenistic myths provided the models. The figure of Christ was formed in the cult and overlaid with the gilded splendour of divinity. It was consolidated in the endless dogmatic battles of the early church.

I hardly dare to think further. Have I bound myself in faith and trust to a figure who does not exist and never existed in this form? A figure who at best exists only in human heads and hearts, a figure which they themselves have created?

Yet even if the Christ of faith has been 'only' formed in the human heart, he is nevertheless so good and so true, and so near to God, that anyone who is seeking the good and the true, anyone who is seeking God, is time and again gripped by him. And this has happened all down the centuries.

Jesus or Christ?

Who is really normative for me? The poor man from Nazareth who was so full of God that it brought him to the cross? Or the radiant son of God who 'rules and reigns' as the exalted Lord? Jesus or Christ?

If I want to give a spontaneous answer to this question from the heart, without any theological reflection, I have to confess that the man from Nazareth is much closer to me. I feel good with him. I have a feeling of love for him. I am attached to him, though I have to confess that I know very little about him. Perhaps it is only the picture of him that I have made which binds me to him.

The glorious Christ somehow leaves me cold. He intimidates

me. He is too lofty, too artificial, too far removed from my 'ultimate concern'. Unlike the popes and bishops who keep claiming
to be authorized by him, I cannot cope with him as I can with
the human Jesus.

'Stop!,' at this point at least the church theologians say to me.
'Here you are creating an opposition between Jesus and Christ.
You may not do that. It is the testimony of scripture and the
confession of the church that Jesus is the Christ.'

Humanity and divinity?

What the theologians say is right. The basic formula of the
Christian faith is in fact the confession 'Jesus is the Christ', or,
more briefly, 'Jesus Christ'. But the New Testament itself cannot
sustain the unity of the man Jesus with the exalted Christ, the
eternal Son of God: the man Jesus disappears almost completely
behind the exalted Christ and is overlaid by him. The human
Jesus fades into the background. The divine Christ dominates
the scene.

No wonder that the first Christian centuries are dominated by
countless battles over the definition of the relationship between
the humanity of Jesus and his divinity. One need only mention
Arianism, Nestorianism and Monophysitism. Distinctions and
identifications, co-ordinations and subordinations of substances, essences, natures, ways of working and persons, of
human and divine will and knowledge, become more and more
complicated, convoluted and hair-splitting in the late church
fathers and the definitions of the councils.

I am convinced that Jesus himself would not have understood
this theological sophistry about his person and would simply
have shaken his head had he read statements like the following
from the Council of Chalcedon:

'One and the same is Christ, Son, Lord, only-begotten;
acknowledged in two natures unconfusedly, unchangeably,

indivisibly, inseparably; the difference of the natures being in no way removed because of the union, but rather the property of each nature being preserved, and both concurring into one prosopon and one hypostasis.'

Such christological formulae derive from the thought and the questions of late antiquity. They could have been useful for the church of the time in defining the relationship of the man Jesus to the Son of God with the help of the categories of thought at that time. They speak in terms which now have taken on quite another meaning and thus are hardly comprehensible for people of today, even educated people. They give answers to questions from the second to the fifth centuries. Ours are different.

What he means to me

At this point I want to attempt to indicate as simply as possible, without any theological acrobatics, what Jesus means for me personally.

For me Jesus is first of all a human being from whom I can take my bearings. Of all the people I know personally, of all the people known to me from human history, there is no one who can provide a better and more reliable orientation for my thought, judgment and action.

For me Jesus is like a signpost showing the direction when I no longer know which way where to go. I believe that the way that he has shown is one which can lead people to a more humane life, to a life in which more love and peace, more goodness and mercy, more joy and perhaps also more happiness and less evil and suffering, are possible. I believe that the way that Jesus has shown is a way that leads humanity into a more worthwhile future.

For me, Jesus is the criterion of what is to be regarded as truly human. Everything that corresponds to the life, the teaching, the spirit and the character of Jesus is human. He is the true human being. What is truly human can be read off him and his life. What cannot stand before him cannot be regarded as 'human' either. The more it contradicts his example and his character, the more 'inhuman' it becomes.

I believe that Jesus has the power to change people who give themselves to him. For their good. He arouses a readiness to prefer the truth to self-advantage, serving to ruling, reconciliation to victory.

I believe that human life can gain all the greater freedom and attain all the greater humanity, the more it opens itself to his spirit and allows itself to be governed by him. I believe that salvation comes into human life when one relies on him. He encourages me to find my own truth and stand by it. Before him I can accept myself as I am, even with my limitations.

For me, Jesus is judge. For me, what is truly good and what must truly be called evil depends on how he would judge it. Where I recognize that I have acted against his instructions and his character, I know that I have acted falsely and badly, that I have become guilty.

For me, Jesus is Lord. If I allow him to rule over me, precepts, commandments, laws, instructions, even from the church, are not the last norm of my judgment and action. A living person to whom I listen ultimately determines the nature of my action. He is the final authority. This relativizes the authority of generalized moral conventions and the instructions of the church. Submission to his judgment makes me more free, and independent of the judgment of other men and women: more free from the pressure of the social environment, and also independent of the judgment of church opinions.

By Jesus I measure all who claim power and status, even the high and mighty in the state, society and the church. As a rule they do not measure up well and lose significance for me. 'He casts down the mighty from their thrones,' the Magnificat says. That brings freedom. My orientation on Jesus allows me an immediacy to God which does not first need to be communicated by church institutions, offices, authorities, teachings, instructions or rites.

I believe that in his person and his life something of the ground, the meaning, the way and the goal of our whole life has become visible and can be experienced: the truth about human beings, God!

Even if today I see Jesus rather differently from the current understanding of the church, I can still – like Thomas from the Gospel of John – say to him, 'My Lord and my God.' For me you are 'Lord'; for me you are 'God', my 'ultimate concern'.

Perhaps what I am saying here in the context of present-day meanings is not so far removed from what the ancient biblical and ecclesiastical formulae were attempting to express in the context of the meanings of their time.

10

Sacrificed on the cross?

Since the sermons which I heard in my childhood days, since the teachings which I received in my own religious instruction in the village school and later in secondary school, phrases have kept ringing in my ear: 'who has redeemed us from sin by his most precious blood, by his bitter suffering and by his death on the cross'. 'In his blood cleansed from all guilt.' 'The lamb that was slain to reconcile us with God.'

I have meanwhile heard these words a thousand times, in every variation, in every possible context: in hundreds of sermons, in countless prayers in the liturgy, at the baptisms of babies and at funerals, in the Corpus Christi procession and on Easter Eve; in Sunday homilies, in episcopal pastoral letters and in papal addresses. Nevertheless I must honestly confess that I have still not understood precisely what they mean.

Certainly I know their historical background. The notion that guilt can be cleansed only by blood goes far back into an archaic way of thinking. This way of thinking is still alive today in the notions of blood vengeance and clan feuds in southern countries, in duels 'to satisfy honour'. It provided a basis for bloody vengeance and thus became the occasion of countless massacres and wars. The notion that the most serious guilt needs to be atoned for by blood and life even plays a part in the imposition of a death sentence.

Blood!

In a Hindu temple in Nepal I looked on in disgust as hens and lambs were slaughtered and their blood offered to the deities. The history of the religions reeks of blood. Blood was always a quite special drink for the gods. Blood seems to make deities gracious. Not just the blood of innocent sacrificial animals, but also the blood of slain human beings seems to be a welcome drink for them.

It was also blood, the blood of a slaughtered lamb, which the Hebrew slaves in Egypt smeared on the doorposts of their houses at their exodus from Egypt. They were spared by blood when 'the Lord slew all the firstborn in the land of Egypt' (Exod.12.12). Blood liberated and redeemed Israel 'from the slavery of Egypt'. Israel celebrated its Passover each year in memory of this deliverance, liberation and redemption. At the festival the Passover lamb was slain.

Blood atones, blood reconciles, blood purifies, blood delivers, blood liberates, blood . . . redeems.

The blood of the lamb

This Jewish rite of sacrificing a lamb at Passover to commemorate the deliverance from Egyptian slavery became a key for Paul in interpreting the death of Jesus on the cross: 'Christ our Passover lamb has been sacrificed' (I Cor.5.7).

Just as Israel was once delivered and redeemed by the blood of the lamb, so humankind is delivered from the power of sin and death by the blood of Jesus.

In this view Jesus became the 'lamb of God', the 'scapegoat' on whom guilt was laden. What was once brought about by the blood of the sacrificial lamb is now brought about by the blood of Jesus. It atones, it reconciles, it purifies, it delivers, it liberates, it takes away guilt, it redeems. 'You are ransomed with the precious blood of Christ, the lamb without spot or stain' (I Peter 1.18).

This gave birth to a doctrine of sacrifice and redemption which to the present day stands at the centre of Christian doctrine and the church's practice, even more than the teaching and message of Jesus himself.

This is how it sounds in the language of the Catechism:

'Christ's death is both the Paschal sacrifice that accomplishes the definitive redemption of men, through "the Lamb of God, who takes away the sin of the world", and the sacrifice of the New Covenant, which restores man to communion with God by reconciling him to God through the "blood of the covenant, which was poured out for many for the forgiveness of sins"' (1/ no.613).

The death of Jesus – planned by God?

The interpretation of the death of Jesus as an atoning death had grown out of the shock at his crucifixion which his followers had had to work through. Jesus, whom people had believed to be the Messiah who would free Israel, had failed. He had ended up shamefully on the cross like a criminal. His death had shattered all the hopes that had been pinned on him. How could one proclaim to believing Jews a Messiah who had failed and ended on the cross like a criminal?

We find the answer in Paul, and later also in the Gospels: the disastrous event was reinterpreted as a saving event. The crucified Jewish Messiah became the redeemer of all humankind. His death was not a failure; his death was a sacrifice, offered to God in love and obedience. His death lay within the plan of God, whose will it was to redeem humankind from the sovereignty of sin and death.

The depiction of Jesus' passion in the Gospel of John is also stamped by the intention of portraying Jesus as the 'Passover lamb'. That extends as far as the chronology of events.

I doubt whether Jesus willed his death in order to redeem

humankind. His commitment was too centred on the 'children of Israel' for that. Jesus did not sacrifice himself in order to offer an atoning sacrifice to God. He had a different picture of the Father. Jesus suffered death because to the last he stood by his cause, which for him was at the same time God's cause.

Atoning sacrifice – an archaic, pagan notion

At best I can understand the church's theology of sacrifice and redemption as a time-conditioned attempt on the part of early Christians to attribute a God-given meaning to the catastrophic death of Jesus. This interpretation took place with the help of notions which were already present in Jewish thought: the image of the suffering servant of God and the custom of the Passover meal which recalled that Israel was once redeemed from slavery in Egypt by the blood of the Passover lamb.

The religious idea that sacrificial blood reconciles the deity and obliterates guilt, which was widespread at that time, also stands in the background of the New Testament interpretation. Motifs like atoning by a bloody sacrifice, not just by the blood of sacrificial animals but also by human blood shed in honour of the deity, also appear in the myths and sagas of other religions. At any rate the notion of a God killed innocently, whose blood brings salvation to human beings, can be found in the myths of peoples centuries before the death of Jesus. In the religion of Mithras, too, the sacrificial priests poured the blood of a sacrificed bull on believers and thus washed their sins away.

Such notions from the religious environment of the Judaism of the time were transferred to Jesus. Jesus is the lamb of God that takes away the sins of the world. These are time-conditioned magical and mythical interpretations which were understood by the people of that period. They served faith by giving the death of Jesus a divinely-willed meaning. In the secularized world of today, in which such notions of sacrifice no longer play a role, these formulae of the church's faith become empty words, incomprehensible and incredible. They can no longer communicate to present-day men and women what was originally meant by them.

They only have a significance in the ritual language within the church. They degenerate into cultic spells.

'. . . gave his Son'?

According to the Christian doctrine of redemption, 'God so loved the world that he gave his only begotten Son'. So was the cruel death of Jesus on the cross part of God's saving plan? Was the death sentence which Jesus suffered willed by God?

The Catholic Catechism replies with all the clarity than can be desired: 'Jesus' violent death was not the result of chance in an unfortunate coincidence of circumstances, but is part of the mystery of God's plan, as St Peter explains to the Jews of Jerusalem in his first sermon on Pentecost: "This Jesus [was] delivered up according to the definite plan and foreknowledge of God"' (1/ no.599).

While the Catechism goes on to assert in splendid innocence that this does not mean that those who betrayed Jesus were 'merely passive players in a scenario written in advance by God', this church teaching nevertheless makes the Jewish accusers and the Roman executioners God's instruments, and it has God pulling the strings in the background, as their secret accomplice.

Pope John Paul II teaches that Mary stood under her son's cross, 'in keeping with the divine plan . . . joining herself with his sacrifice in her mother's heart, and lovingly consenting to the immolation of this victim, born of her' (1/ no.964).

My God, can't these people see how monstrous this is? Are they so trapped in their system of thought that they've lost all sense of how remote their thinking has become from the message of Jesus?

Abraham's sacrifice

In an official comment on a book by Hans Küng in November 1977 the German bishops compared the action of God in the crucifixion of his only Son Jesus Christ with Abraham's behaviour at the sacrificing of his son Isaac. Abraham seemed to them to be only a 'pale foreshadowing', because he did not go through with the slaughter of his son. But, the bishops went on, 'The heavenly Father does not stop, he gives his only Son, his most beloved, and therefore himself, for us' (cf.17/ 329, 346).

Probably one of the most significant features of the notion of God which developed among the people of Israel was that the God of Israel scorned human sacrifice. With a few exceptions mentioned in the Bible which are also repudiated with abhorrence, Israel offered no human sacrifices to its God. Thus Israel's God stood quite alone among the deities of the surrounding peoples.

The famous story of Abraham relates how he was willing to sacrifice his son Isaac to the Lord. The event certainly never took place as narrated in the Bible. The story does not describe a historical event but reflects Israel's clash with the practice of human sacrifice in neighbouring religions. And its unknown author puts the answer to which Israel's reflection led in the mouth of an angel of God: 'Do not lay your hand on the boy or do anything to him' (Gen.22.12).

Israel's God does not want the sacrifice of a son, or any human sacrifice. Instead of this Abraham offers a ram.

What Jesus understood by sacrifice

The slaughter of sacrificial animals, primarily of lambs, was customary in all Mediterranean and Near Eastern pastoral cultures, including Israel up to the time of the destruction of the temple by the Romans. However, the prophets already criticized sacrifices and burnt offerings. 'I do not want sacrifices but love,' says God in Hosea (6.6).

Jesus also quotes this saying by the prophet (Matt.9.13). God does not want sacrifices but a change of heart, repentance, justice, mercy. Jesus' understanding of sacrifice stands in the prophetic line. For Jesus, sacrifice means loving devotion to God, doing the will of the Father, living according to God's will. In this way 'sin', the failure to be in harmony with God, is overcome: not through the shedding of blood, not through the slaughter of animals and human beings, not through dying, but through repentance, love and forgiveness. The God of Jesus needs no bloody satisfaction to forgive a sin. Has the prodigal son been overlooked in the construction of the Christian doctrine of redemption?

In the face of the message of Jesus and the prophets, the church's theory of sacrifice seems like an atavistic lapse into an archaic form of religious thought. It falls far short of the prophets, indeed even of Abraham; it goes back into the time of child sacrifice. In the Abraham story the sacrificing of human blood is superseded and replaced with animal sacrifice. And in the prophets justice and mercy are preferred to the slaughtering of animals. This is truly a great step forward in the evolution of human religious consciousness.

However, in the church's interpretation of the death of Jesus the step leads in the opposite direction. The sacrifice of the only son replaces the slaughter of sacrificial animals.

Not Jesus' image of God

Jesus had depicted his God in the image of the gracious father. His was a God who rushes towards his prodigal son without asking anything of him, takes him in his arms and forgives him unconditionally. However, it was not Jesus' picture of God that became the centre of the church's faith and worship, but the pagan-mythical picture of a deity who had been infinitely insulted by the disobedience of a single individual and who could be reconciled only by human blood, the atoning death of his own Son.

'Salvation' does not come into the world from the rule of God which Jesus announced. Human redemption from guilt and alienation from God was not grounded in God's care for men and women, but in the sacrificial victim on the cross, which was 'within God's plan'.

It was not the message of Jesus but the doctrine of his atoning sacrificial death which became the centre of the church's faith. For this doctrine of redemption ensures the church its significance, its status and its power more than the message of Jesus. As the Catechism teaches, '. . . the saving mission entrusted by the Father to his incarnate Son was committed to the apostles and through them to their successors' (1/ no.1120).

Anyone to whom the stewardship and distribution of the temporal and eternal salvation of humankind has been entrusted in this way almost automatically gets a central key position between God and humankind. The 'fruits of redemption' which Jesus has earned through his death on the cross are administered and apportioned by those who hold office in the church. So I can well understand why the church has put this doctrine of redemption at the centre of its teaching and its worship.

The administration of salvation – according to existing regulations

The administration of the 'fruits of redemption' in practice amounted to the forgiveness of sins in the confessional. But it was impossible even for the bishops to fail to see that the sacrament of penance no longer enjoyed any great popularity among the faithful. The number of penitents had declined rapidly.

This fact led many pastors and theologians to rethink the sacrament of penance and reflect again on what Jesus taught about the forgiveness of sins. Jesus did not call on people to

make their confessions. Rather, he called on them to change
their lives. He preached that a new beginning becomes possible
for those who desist from evil and direct their life anew by God.
That is truly a good and helpful message.

However, according to the message and teaching of Jesus,
God's forgiveness is not bound up with church procedures;
Jesus' only condition is a change of heart, a renewal of disposition, an honest readiness for a new beginning. Jesus certainly never instituted auricular confession in which sins are
exclusively forgiven by a Catholic priest.

At that time many people again became aware of what was
originally the core of truth in the forgiveness of sins by the
church: forgiveness is to live on and have an effect in the community of those who believe in Christ. Those who have incurred
such guilt that it separates them from the community of fellow-
Christians are nevertheless to be accepted back and forgiven, if
they distance themselves from their guilt and change their lives.

From this new reflection on the New Testament foundations
of the forgiveness of sins, many attempts developed at that time
to put new emphases in pastoral care. Auricular confession was
recognized as only one of the many possible forms of conversion
and forgiveness, although a high pastoral value was still
attached to it.

A personal return to God, combined with a request for
forgiveness from those who had been wronged, was again
emphasized more strongly. Similarly, an attempt was made to
revive an age-old church practice, the penitential service with a
common confession of guilt by the community and a general
promise of God's forgiveness by the priest.

The representatives of the episcopate frowned on the efforts
made by the pastors. These efforts provoked their distrust and
disapproval more than anything else. A degree by the Vicar
General appeared in the official diocesan journal which pointed
out that according to existing regulations the forgiveness of sins
took place only in sacramental penance. The document actually
used the words 'according to existing regulations'. I can still

remember how perplexed and irritated I was when I read it. I once again became aware how far official church thought had departed from its origin in the preaching of Jesus.

God's forgiveness as proclaimed by Jesus is distributed 'in accordance with existing regulations'. Here is the administration of salvation in a legalistic form. However, anyone who knows how much power over people has accrued to the church and how strongly the church influences society simply through the confessional will understand the Vicar General's concern.

The cross in life – pleasing to God?

Since – according to the teaching of the church – 'the bitter suffering and most holy cross of Jesus proved to be pleasing to God and brought salvation, the suffering and cross of ordinary Christians must also be pleasing to God and brings salvation'. Indeed! The Catechism of the German Bishops follows this logic: 'His (Jesus') will is that those who first benefit from his redeeming sacrifice should take part in this sacrifice.' 'There is no other ladder than the cross by which to ascend into heaven' (11/ no.191).

I received a letter from a priest in Spain who used to be my children's religious education teacher and who often stayed in our house. Now he holds a leading position in Opus Dei, but I still have a high personal regard for him because he is an honest man with a 'pure heart'. On the letterhead was the slogan of Escrivá, the founder of Opus Dei: '*In laetitia, nulla dies sine Cruce.*' 'In joy, no day without a cross.'

Now it may well be that in my life, too, a time will come when no day passes without pain. And I do not know how I shall cope with that. I shall have to put up with it then, because I shall have no alternative. But is that a 'joy'? Is that willed by God?

A God who enjoys the suffering of his creatures must be a malicious God. He is hardly any different from the cruel deities of prehistoric times to whom human torment was a welcome sacrificial food. He is a perverse God. That is not the God of Jesus. From Jesus I get another picture of God, a God who wants human well-being, happiness, joy, wholeness; a God who does not want human suffering; a God who wants to free people from suffering.

Eugen Drewermann's Giordano Bruno says: 'My main objection to the Christ of the Christians is that his instinct is to claim that to flee pain and seek happiness is contrary to God, and he has brought human beings a God who uses the suffering of the innocent as atonement for his avenging justice. No one can ever commit a worse sin against human beings and against God' (3/ 146).

Note that Giordano Bruno says this of 'the Christ of the Christians', and not of Jesus.

Offering sacrifices?

The doctrine of the atoning sacrificial death which derives from archaic pagan notions led to the cross becoming the real sign of Christian faith. Certainly one can interpret the cross as a sign of sacrificial love, and thus it points to the centre of Christianity. But does the cross really manifest the essence of love? Aren't the emphases shifted one-sidedly to sacrifice and pain?

Certainly love is ready also to offer sacrifices, to make renunciations, to put its own desire for happiness in the background and even to take pain upon itself for the sake of the loved one – but this is not sacrifice, renunciation, pain for its own sake. These are not the aim; they have no intrinsic value. From the perspective of the God of Jesus they even seem to me to be non-values. For the God of Jesus wants human well-being, joy, peace, happiness. The God of Jesus does not want the cross. He does not want pain; he seeks the avoidance of pain and the healing of wounds. He does not want suffering. He wants suffering, distress, misery, hatred and enmity to be overcome; he wants tears to be dried.

The acceptance of sacrifice and pain can only have a value pleasing to God if they are accepted for the sake of love, for the sake of the good that is to be achieved, and not as an end in themselves. To offer sacrifice is not in itself pleasing to God. God is pleased if we are good to others, if we are there when we are needed, if we help one another to serve and to forgive. At any rate, that is how I have understood the message of Jesus.

Now – after writing these notes – I can understand better why I have never really been able to make anything of the dogmatic and liturgical formulae about Jesus 'who cleanses us from all guilt by his blood' and 'has redeemed us from sin on the cross'. The church's doctrine of sacrifice and redemption does not fit Jesus. I have never been able to accept it 'in the spirit of Jesus'.

11

Risen from the tomb?

Resurrection – no return to former life

Travelling through Turkey with my two daughters, who were then around sixteen or seventeen, I arrived at Pamukale, ancient Hierapolis. Near the famous terraces through which warm water flows down from the calcareous springs, there is a necropolis, a city of the dead with hundreds of ancient stone graves. A sarcophagus hewn from a block of stone with a slab lying above it reminded me of the pictures of the resurrection by Matthias Grünewald, Albrecht Altdorfer and other late mediaeval painters. I couldn't resist the temptation to persuade one of my daughters to get into the tomb, so that she could rise from it with a victorious gesture 'like Jesus'. The picture is still in the album of this trip.

I allowed myself this joke because already at that time I knew that the resurrection of Jesus couldn't be imagined like that. Jesus didn't rise from the dead as a dead person might suddenly come to life again and rise from the tomb. Almost all important biblical theologians now agree on that. Jesus did not return to his old corporeal life.

If there is any truth in talk about the resurrection of Jesus it is certainly not to be understood so superficially, but far more deeply.

Resurrection – only one of many images

We find the earliest documentation of Christian belief in the resurrection in Paul. 'Christ died for our sins, according to the scriptures. He was buried and rose the third day, according to the scriptures. He appeared to Cephas, then to the Twelve. Last of all also to me' (I Cor.15.3-8). This formula at the same time contains the heart of the message which Paul proclaimed in constantly new variants: the cross was not the end of Jesus. Jesus did not fail as Messiah. He conquered on the cross. Everything that happened, happened 'according to the scriptures'. God confirmed the crucified Jesus after his death as Messiah.

Paul expresses this message in many different images: God has exalted him . . . made him Lord . . . appointed him heir. He was transfigured . . . transformed. He appeared. God raised him. He is risen.

Of all these different pictures which surround and interpret the same experience, only the one mentioned last, that of resurrection, has left its stamp on the faith of Christianity. It determines our understanding of 'resurrection', probably because it is the most vivid. The image of raising, in which God is the active one, is later intensified so that it becomes the image of rising, in which Jesus himself performs the powerful act. In the four Gospels this image was later developed and graphically presented in narrative form by the stories of the empty tomb.

'A historical fact'?

It is the unanimous opinion of almost all leading Christian theologians, Catholic and Protestant, that the stories about the empty tomb do not describe a real historical event. The accounts in the four Gospels are too contradictory. More than two hundred years ago, in a work published by Lessing after his death, Reimarus pointed out the many inconsistencies.

The event of the resurrection is not to be understood historically as the actual revival of a corpse, even through the 'empty
tomb'. The narratives of the empty tomb, the women who went
to the tomb and the angels who gave them the news of the resurrection are legendary stories, not descriptions of historical
events. They do not depict actual events which form the basis
for belief in the resurrection; rather, they proclaim and make
vivid the Easter faith of the earliest church which had already
been effective for decades.

Even information which seems so incidental, like 'on the third
day', is not chronological information. This expression is
a 'symbolic means of theological expression' to which the present chairman of the German conference of bishops, Karl
Lehmann, once drew attention when he was still writing as a
professor. Theologians who are aware of the lack of tangible
historical facts in the resurrection narratives nevertheless
attempt to put this lack on the credit side by referring, as Karl
Lehmann does, to the mysterious character of the Easter event:
'However, the event of the resurrection of Jesus completely
escapes all human notions and thus also all earthly measures of
time' (16/ 66).

Contrary to all the insights of present-day biblical criticism,
the Catechism still deals with the Easter stories as though they
were factual accounts: 'Given these testimonies, Christ's resurrection cannot be interpreted as something outside the physical
order, and it is impossible not to acknowledge it as a historical
fact' (1/ no.643).

Unimaginable

Totally unenlightened, I must simply ask: if according to the
teaching of the papal Catechism the resurrection belongs in the
'physical order', how am I to imagine this 'historical fact'? If
something belongs to the 'physical order', then it is subject to
unavoidable physical conditions. So did the crucified Jesus rise

bodily from the tomb? Did he go around on his bodily feet, obeying the 'physical order' of gravity? Did the witnesses whom he chose in fact see him with their eyes according to the 'physical order', i.e. through the physical medium of light waves? Did they speak to him through the physical medium of sound waves? If something takes place according to the 'physical order', it is unavoidably subject to the biological constraints of metabolism. May I imagine that in quite specific terms in the case of the risen Jesus?

'Stop!', say the theologians of the church to my attempt to understand. 'Your thought and your questions are quite wrong. You cannot imagine the resurrection at all. It is unimaginable. It is a mystery. Moreover Jesus now had a transfigured body. His corporeality was transformed.' Aha! So that's it.

The Archbishop of Paderborn tells me: 'No one saw the event of the resurrection. It remains a mystery. Nor will I even attempt to imagine it.'

The great phrase 'the mystery of the resurrection', God's greatest miracle, which transcends all human understanding, intimidates me. I hardly dare to ask what it means. The many stereotyped church formulae with which the resurrection is spoken of conceal and obscure more from me than they reveal and illuminate.

Linguistic images which surround an experience

None of the expressions and linguistic formulae in which the New Testament speaks of the Easter event are descriptions of historical events which can be perceived by the senses. They are figurative expressions.

Resurrection, exaltation, appearance, transformation of his life, transfiguration of his body, exaltation to be Lord, appointed Son – all these formulae are linguistic images which surround one and the same 'experience' and attempt to interpret and express it.

Indeed, even phrases like '. . . ascended to heaven', '. . . sits at the right hand of God', 'put all things under his feet' and '. . . among us through his spirit' belong among the images which members of the earliest communities found and used to interpret and express an impressive experience which was particularly important to them, the so-called Easter experience.

The images of resurrection, exaltation, ascension, sending of the Spirit, mean one and the same thing. Even the image of virgin birth in the Christmas stories is a development which illustrates the Easter faith.

The truth must lie deeper

Once I have discovered, with the help of the biblical theologians, that the expressions 'resurrection' or 'appearance' are images which interpret and illlustrate an experience, the 'Easter experience', I can no longer imagine the resurrection of Jesus to mean that the disciples saw a risen Jesus with their eyes, heard him with their ears, or touched him with their hands. That would once again be to misunderstand a powerful, deep image as a miraculous fact and to seek and to defend the real truth contained in the images in the wrong place, namely in allegedly external events. Like most theologians, I must bid farewell to any understanding of the Easter experience as an empirical experience of external events.

Because of this, I also cannot accept the attempts at a 'natural' explanation which are offered e.g. by A.N.Wilson, when he conjectures that after the death of Jesus the disciples had seen his brother James, and confused him with Jesus (25). Nor can I follow the explanation of H.von Mendelsohn, that Jesus had not been completely dead when he was taken down from the cross, that he had been nursed back to health by the women and later made contact with some of his disciples, the marks of his wounds still visible, though this would have a degree of plausibility (24). It is on the same level as the suspicion of the Jews that the disciples had secretly removed the body of Jesus, namely the level of external facts.

The 'truth' of the Easter faith must lie deeper.

'Inner experiences'?

Or was it an inner experience in the sense of an 'inward illumination' brought about by God?

Such attempts at an explanation of the Easter experience are made by many theologians, especially Protestant theologians. They attempt to avoid the contradictions in the miraculous facts which they know about by transferring the miracle inwards: God brought it about that the divinity and messiahship of Jesus dawned on the disciples, that in a sudden illumination they became aware that Jesus lives on. 'Jesus rose in the faith of the community,' they say. I find these attempts to explain the Easter experiences easier to understand and they cause me less difficulty. But I am not content with them either.

Forms of sudden knowledge, flashes of knowledge, are well known to psychology and epistemology, and can have a natural explanation without necessarily having to be referred to the influence of a God who communicates himself. Specifically in the sphere of religion, not only famous founders of religions like Buddha and Muhammad appeal to such 'inner illumination'. Joan of Arc refers to an illumination and like the children of Fatima and Lourdes speaks of 'appearances'. Many founders of sects and converts report experiences in which in a flash an uncertain hypothesis becomes unconditional certainty. I cannot recognize any experience which would be sufficient to base belief in the resurrection on in such inner illuminations. They are the subject-matter of psychology, not theology.

What really happened?

So I continue to ask: what kind of experiences at that time, almost two thousand years ago, led to the origin of belief in a resurrection of Jesus? What really happened then?

Of course I don't know. No one knows precisely, not even the pope and the bishops.

I know how uncertain the ground becomes if one attempts to reconstruct a historical event from biblical sources. So I will only attempt to give a few pointers to the direction in which my conjectures go. I have no proofs to put on the table. However, I feel that my conjecture is much more likely to correspond to the historical event than many other explanations that I have heard in the church. My question now is quite simply what could really have taken place historically.

After the death of Jesus on the cross, everything collapsed for those who had pinned their hopes on him. 'We had hoped that he was the one to liberate Israel,' the disciples lament in Luke (24.21), thus expressing the disappointment of all those who had shared their belief that Jesus was the Messiah. In the strictest sense of the term they had had to 'bury' their hope in someone who had opened up the way to a better future for them. He had failed as Messiah. His cause, in which they had so trusted, seemed lost for all time.

However, in the course of the period after Jesus' death his followers had another experience: the effect which had emanated from Jesus during his lifetime by no means ended with his death. On the contrary, it continued and was even intensified. Even after his death something emanated from his figure which could take hold of people and change them. This Jesus had really set something in motion which was effective beyond his death. It was almost as though he were not lying dead in the tomb but was still alive and working among them, more powerfully than before.

Confirmed as Messiah

In fact Jesus' followers had to see God himself at work in Jesus' ongoing activity: God had confirmed Jesus as Messiah. To have believed and hoped in him had not been a mistake. Jesus had been right. And they had also been right to follow him: he was indeed the Messiah. The doubts in Jesus which had oppressed his disciples at his death had been overcome. New certainty, new hope, new faith were there.

Now people saw his death on the cross in another light, and in this light it was reinterpreted. Jesus' death on the cross had not been a manifest failure which shattered their hopes; his death became the sign of God's love for humankind and his obedience to God. The crucifixion was no longer a catastrophe; it became an ingredient of the divine redemption from the power of sin and death. The shameful death of Jesus on the cross between criminals had not put an end to the 'cause of Jesus', the dawning of the kingly rule of God, but had helped it to break through. The cross became a sign of victory; the battered man who died in torment on this cross became the victor over death.

'He was obedient to death, even the death of the cross,' Paul now says. 'Therefore God has exalted him above all. Every knee shall bow to him and every tongue confess that Jesus Christ is Lord' (Phil.2.6-11). These words denote precisely what at another point is described as 'resurrection from the dead', only with another image and in another context.

It was natural for the thought and imagination of that time to express and interpret the continuing activity of Jesus in the linguistic imagery that we find in the New Testament: 'Jesus lives. God has raised him and given him new life. Jesus has risen. The tomb is empty.'

The faith of the disciples had literally brought him back from the tomb. If we are in search of historically tangible facts on which Christian belief in the resurrection is based, then these are more likely to be found in the realm of suchlike events.

Raisings of the dead – no unusual idea at that time

The images and notions in which the earliest church expressed its faith in the divine confirmation of the crucified Jesus as Messiah did not need to be invented; they were already there, both in Judaism and in the Hellenistic environment. They need only to be taken up and adopted.

For the people of that time, there was nothing extraordinary in the idea that a person had been roused again from the sleep of death. The boundaries between the possible and the impossible were not as well-defined as they are in our present-day view of the world, with its scientific stamp. Stories of miraculous raisings of the dead kept circulating, and people had no difficulty in believing them. Babylonian myths call some deities 'revivers of the dead'. The Gospels also narrate Jesus' raisings of the dead: Jairus's daughter, the young man of Nain, his friend Lazarus.

We can see from this how easy it was for people at that time to believe that a dead person could be brought back to life. In Matthew, Jesus even commands the disciples to 'Heal the sick and raise the dead' (10.8).

A mythical image?

It is related of a contemporary of Jesus, the philosopher Apollonius of Tyana, that in Rome he raised to life a girl who was about to be buried, and that after himself suffering the death penalty he rose from the dead and ascended into heaven. Already three hundred years before Jesus it was reported of Pythagoras that he had been persecuted, condemned, killed, had descended to the underworld and had then rose again from the dead.

I have already mentioned that the image of a slain divine saviour who rose from the dead and returned to heaven was a basic element in many myths of antiquity. This image has its origin in the vegetation deities in whom the seasonal dying and rising again in nature was divinized.

In Syria Adonis, in Phrygia Attis, in Egypt Osiris, in Thrace Dionysus were worshipped as deities. They were all raised from the dead to new life. The cult of the Babylonian god Tammuz, who rose from the dead, was also known in Jerusalem. The cult of the vegetation god Sandan is attested from Tarsus, Paul's birthplace. There was a festival on which his death and his resurrection were celebrated. His cult may also have been known to Paul (cf. 7/ 64, 70, 90, 106, 193).

Such myths were still very much alive in the Hellenistic environment of Judaism at the time of the earliest church. They were told among the people and were also known to the Hellenistic Jews. The cults with which they were associated rivalled the Christ cult in early Christianity.

So the question arises: is it really eccentric to consider the possibility that the mythical motif of a god who was killed and raised to life again became a picture by which the early Christians could express their faith in the messiahship of Jesus?

Not seeking the truth in the historical

The Gospels relate that Jesus rose from the dead, which is what the myths also relate of their heroes and sons of god. I must now go on to ask: could it perhaps be that both statements have a common origin, a common root, a common source, and express a common truth? In that case the truth about the resurrection of Jesus would need to be sought not in history, not in a single event in the past, but in something which is common to human beings over time and their different ways of thinking.

I do not get any further if I seek the truth of the resurrection of Jesus only in historical events, whether or not they may have occurred. I also feel this in my reflections while writing these 'notes'. But if I also look at the resurrection existentially, new possibilities of understanding and of faith open up to me.

For example I can understand why there is already mention of resurrection in the mythical religions before Jesus and outside Christianity. What would then be being spoken of in both cases would not be an individual miraculous historical event but a truth which is experienced time and again by human beings, beyond the limits of particular times and religions. The myths and religions have simply attached this 'truth' to individuals and illlustrated it.

Passing away – changing – rising again

Everything that is, is at some time and in some way subject to decline, decay and death. But this passing away is not the end. It is part of a process of transformation. It is the beginning of a new origin in changed form, a 'new creation'. Human beings have been able to experience this all over the world since the beginning of human history, at all times and in all areas. It is a basic truth of all existence.

It is already visible in the realm of nature, in the seasonal dying off of vegetation and its 'resurrection' by the power of the sun in the spring. It is no coincidence that the mythical deities which died and rose were originally vegetation deities. Human history shows how all social structures – families, clans, dynasties, rulers, states – flourish, perish and rise again in a changed form; this is an experience of the same 'truth' of existence.

The basic law of passing away, changing and rising again is also recognized by the modern natural sciences. Evolutionary biology knows that there can be no further and higher development of life without death. There is no Easter without Good Friday. Without death, without transformation, life would have remained unicellular and would never have produced the variety of plants and animals, nor human beings. Life constantly arises anew and develops further only in a dialectical interplay with death.

Modern physics has also demonstrated this basic law of

decline, transformation and new creation in the material sphere. It applies in both the macrocosm and the microcosm. New stars in the universe come into being from the matter and the energy of old stars which have 'died'. Like the whole of the Milky Way, our sun, to the radiation of whose energy we owe the origin of all life on earth, once 'arose anew' from transformations of cosmic matter and energy. And one day, in many billions of years, it too will experience its Good Friday, so that by passing away new stars may arise.

The same thing is true in the microcosmic sphere of atoms and molecules, neutrons and electrons, and elementary particles. Here too the law of passing away, transformation and rising again applies in a changed form. Over many billions of years the constant processes of transformation in the sub-atomic sphere led beyond the material sphere to chemical processes, and from these to higher biological, psychological and spiritual developments. Only in this way could human beings come into being along with their religion: through death, transformation, resurrection.

Could it not be that this universal basic law of the world which is at work and can be experienced in all events in the world is the 'truth' that is the theme of Easter faith and already before this in many myths?

The existential 'truth' of Easter faith

Passing away and becoming new, dying and rising, are funda-mental processes of the whole of life. Nothing new comes into being without something old perishing. The passing away of the old is the presupposition of the coming into being of the new. It is important for the way in which we cope both individually and collectively with the experience of decline, passing away and death in each individual. This insight helps us to deal with such experience, and gives hope that death does not have the last word. It gives strength for survival. I suppose that it was such universal human experiences of life which found an account not only in myths but also in belief in the resurrection of Jesus.

The Easter faith's message of the resurrection of Jesus sums up figuratively the human experience of the passing of life through death into new transformed life. 'Unless a grain of wheat falls into the earth and dies, it remains alone; but if it dies, it brings forth much fruit' (John 12.24). Here I see the existential, human truth of the Easter faith.

The Easter message can be an encouragement to endure the journey through the night, in trust that the darkness will be lit up beyond the night. It is a promise grounded in experience that forgiveness is possible beyond guilt, and new love beyond hatred. It can give hope in the tribulation of suffering and death that salvation is possible beyond suffering and new life beyond death.

Experiences of love

The deeper existential truth of talk of death, transformation and resurrection to new life can also become visible when one interprets it in terms of inter-personal experiences.

For example, what resurrection means can dawn on lovers who have been driven out of a 'paradise' because guilt destroyed their love, when they experience that even a love which is dead and already buried can be raised to new life. They experience 'resurrection' when they experience a love which is greater and more powerful than guilt. Anyone who has experienced the 'hell' in which a human being can find himself or herself through the death of a love also knows of the 'heaven' which opens up again when the love rises to new life.

As though touched by a magic wand, not only the biblical image of the resurrection but also the images of paradise and the fall, the descent of Jesus into hell and his resurrection, suddenly take on a quite new meaning which we can grasp and follow if we see them from the perspective of basic existential human experiences. They cause difficulties for faith as miraculous historical events 'according to the physical order' which must be firmly held to be true. But now all at once they indicate a deep truth about human beings and life which we can not only regard as true but also accept in faith.

Resurrection also takes place where a buried hope revives and gains strength, where those who have been divided come together again, where enmity turns to friendship and hatred to love. Resurrection takes place where a new future opens up for the desperate, where in the darkness of a hopeless situation a light shines and points a new way.

'. . . it puts death to shame'

Easter Day. This morning a thought suddenly came to me during the Easter mass in church which I want to add here. It came during an Easter hymn which goes, 'There we see the power of his deity, it puts death to shame'.

There is a real and highly effective cause of resurrection faith which lies in the human soul: anxiety about our own death. The biological drive for survival with which we are equipped and which we share with the animals exerts pressure beyond the frontier of death. But unlike the the animals, we know that the power of death cannot be averted or conquered. We may hope that death does not speak the last word about our life, that there is a power which is greater than that of death, a power which also grants us life; even beyond inevitable death.

And only a God can have this power. 'There we see the power of his deity, it puts death to shame.' I ask myself whether faith in God who rose again from the dead is a projection from the depths of the human soul. If one unites with this God one can have hope, hope that at some point after death one will oneself enter a new life through the door which he has opened.

Perhaps the existential root of that truth which is proclaimed in the resurrection of the dead lies here.

Resurrection – a process?

Another thought came to me in this connection. The great majority of present-day theologians think that the 'Easter event' was the cause of the origin of belief in the divinity of Jesus.

But couldn't it have been the other way round? The progressive divinization of Jesus in the years after his death also produced belief in the resurrection. In that case the resurrection faith could be a mythical development and legendary illustration of the faith in Jesus' divinity which arose in the years after his death.

We always imagine the event which is described in the New Testament with the word 'resurrection' to have taken place only a few days after the death of Jesus. But not least as a result of the admirable investigation by the chairman of the German conference of bishops, we know, as I have already mentioned, that the detail 'on the third day' is not a piece of chronological information but a detail of symbolic theology. The 'Easter event' could also have been a process which lasted over many years, perhaps over decades: a process of the progressive divinization of Jesus which found vivid figurative expression in the Easter stories. If it was believed that Jesus was a God or a son of God, then it was almost compulsory to believe that his divine Father had not left him in the tomb.

This idea only occurred to me today. I have never read it anywhere. It is probably just one of the many attempts at an explanation. The significance that Jesus has for me does not become any less if today I attempt to see the resurrection faith in a different way.

No answer?

I read these last notes aloud to my wife. She asked, 'Are you really convinced that what you have written is true?'

'No,' I replied, 'I'm not sure. But of all the possible ways of understanding what resurrection means, they are the ones that say most to me at the moment.'

She said, 'Isn't what is left too little?'

I replied, 'My faith in Jesus doesn't depend on whether Jesus rose from the tomb after his death and appeared bodily to his disciples, whether he spoke, ate and drank with them. My faith doesn't depend on miracles. On the contrary. In this way the Easter faith seems to me to be meaningful and true in a new way, as I attempt to see the resurrection of Jesus differently and to understand it more deeply.'

'And how?,' asked my wife.

'That's what I'm looking for all the time,' I replied.

'Stop bothering me with these questions,' she said. 'You won't find any answer. Enough for today. Let's go to Pinocchio's for a pizza.'

Ascended into heaven?

Jerusalem 1966. I had climbed the Mount of Olives. Here, I had been told, a church stands on the place from which Jesus ascended into heaven. In it they showed me a bit of rock on which one could still see the footprints which Jesus had left behind. At that time, I didn't yet know much about biblical criticism. Nevertheless it seemed to me incredible. I had read nothing in the Bible about Jesus leaving footprints behind.

Meanwhile, however, I have come to recognize that there was never an ascension as it is depicted in Acts and in the Gospel of Luke, whether on the Mount of Olives or elsewhere. The ascension, too, is not a historical fact but an image by which the earliest church expressed and proclaimed its belief in the exaltation of the crucified Messiah and his confirmation by God; in literary terms it is a legend.

In the geocentric picture of the world current at that time it was imagined that the sphere of God, heaven, lay above the disc of the earth. Because the pious Jew was reluctant to speak the name 'God', the word heaven became a substitute for God. The formula 'Jesus has ascended into heaven' does not describe a first space journey, nor a physical exaltation of the body of Jesus into the clouds. It would be more meaningful today to translate it with a phrase like, 'Jesus was wholly accepted into communion with God'. Thus the image of the ascension basically says the same thing as the images of 'resurrection' or 'exaltation'. Easter and Ascension are one and the same.

At that time 'ascension into heaven' was by no means an impossible idea. If the sphere of the divine, heaven, was a vault immediately above the earth, people of that time could easily imagine how an important person could rise to heaven after his death.

Something of this sort was related of many mythical figures like Heracles, Attis and Mithras, or even important people like Homer and Caesar. The Old Testament also speaks of an ascension, in the case of the prophet Elijah.

In the New Testament, only Acts and the Gospel of Luke relate the ascension. A mention of the ascension at the end of the Gospel of Mark has been recognized to be 'inauthentic', a later appendix. In Luke the ascension takes place on the day of Jesus' resurrection, in Bethany; in Acts forty days later, from the Mount of Olives.

The time of Jesus is ending

If the ascension was originally merely another image for expressing belief in Jesus' resurrection, in the later understanding of the church it increasingly became an independent miraculous historical event. That may have been because the resurrection of Jesus was also increasingly understood as a miraculous event of history. The risen Jesus could not have wandered around on earth for all time with a transfigured body, especially as no one ever saw him (apart, of course, from the forerunners of the episcopate).

The historical Jesus had long since been forced into the background by the 'Christ of faith', whose visible body was the church. It was better to appeal to him than to Jesus and his teaching. So what was to be done with the risen Jesus? It was best to let him return whence he came, to heaven.

The reaction of the Grand Inquisitor to Jesus' return to the world dominated by the church, in Dostoievsky's legend of the same name in *The Brothers Karamazov*, is worth noting. How would the Vatican react today if Jesus suddenly stood there and requested an audience with the pope? The unease of the papal court would be as great as the wonderment of Jesus at what these people were teaching and doing in his name.

Ascension? The time of Jesus of Nazareth ended. The rule of the exalted Christ began. And with it the rule of the church.

12

Enlightened by the Spirit

The church – founded by Jesus?

Certainly it cannot be disputed that the church in some way goes back to Jesus. Without Jesus' appearance and activity, no religious community would have arisen which still kept gathering in his name after his death, which expanded and finally developed into a new religion, Christianity.

But there are considerable doubts as to whether this was Jesus' intention. Jesus certainly did not want to found a new religion which detached itself from Judaism. His activity was directed towards the renewal of Israel. He was a pious Jew who thought, prayed, taught, lived and died within his Jewish religion.

Jesus proclaimed the imminent end of the present world and the dawn of a new rule of God over Israel. He called on Israel to repent and wanted to renew Israel's relationship with its God. That alone would already have prevented him from wanting to found a world-wide church which set itself apart from Judaism and would last until 'the end of time'. His gaze was directed towards the deliverance of Israel in the face of the imminent end and not towards the establishment of a lasting church with its centre in Rome, the pope at its head and its goal in an eschatological fulfilment.

Even after Jesus' death, his apostles and disciples still felt themselves to be believing Jews. The Bible of the Jews, the Old Testament, was also their Bible, and governed their view of Jesus and his fate. Jesus did not choose and send out the twelve apostles as precursors of future Catholic bishops. In the New Testament, the 'Twelve' stand for the twelve tribes of Israel. They have been sent 'to the lost sheep of Israel', in order to call them together as a new Israel under the rule of God.

It also seems to me to be questionable whether Jesus, who as a prophetic charismatic dissociated himself from any institution, and was also critical, indeed dismissive, of the Jewish priestly caste, its piety, its cultic practices and its claim to rule, could have founded a new institution which is controlled and shaped by a priestly hierarchy.

I have my doubts whether Jesus wanted and founded this church.

Two kinds of theologies

I read an interview with the well-known biblical theologian Hermann Haag. He was asked whether Jesus founded the church. 'All theologians today are agreed that Jesus of Nazareth did not want to found a church,' he replied.

'Really all of them? Including the bishops?'

'Yes, including the bishops, though of course they won't concede that. Unfortunately there are two kinds of theology in our church: one for the initiated and one for the dumb. That for the initiated is taught at the universities, and that for the dumb is preached from the pulpits' (9/ 27).

'You are Peter . . .'

If Jesus did not intend to found a church, it is also extremely doubtful whether he spoke the famous words to Peter (Matt.16.18) which today adorn the cupola of St Peter's in Rome: 'You are Peter, the rock, and on this rock I will build my church.' With good reason, the majority of biblical theologians regard this saying as a later 'community formation', i.e. words which came into being in the earliest church, often many years after the death of Jesus, and which were subsequently put into his mouth. The background to these words may lie in arguments between individual communities about the rank and priority of their leaders. The pre-eminence of Peter, who had probably already played a leading role among the apostles during the lifetime of Jesus, and was dominant in Jewish Christian communities after the death of Jesus, was emphasized with these words. Only the Gospel of Matthew, which, as is well known, was composed in Jewish-Christian communities, mentions this promise to Peter. The other Gospels know nothing of it. Moreover, the authority of the Bishop of Rome to lead the world church has nothing to do with this saying.

However, as bishop of Rome the pope still bases his seniority over all other bishops and his authority to lead the whole church on it. Historically, though, it is still highly uncertain whether Peter was ever in Rome and whether he really was the first bishop of the Roman community.

Pentecost?

The Acts of the Apostles relates that at the Jewish feast of Pentecost a roaring like a mighty storm suddenly arose, and tongues as of fire descended on 'Peter and his brothers', who were assembled in a house.

All the signs are that this is not the depiction of a historical event. Rather, it is a figurative illustration of the faith of the earliest community that the crucified Jesus is the Messiah, filled with the Spirit by God, who even after his death continues to be active in the community of people who believe in him. The Pentecost narrative is a figurative development of the Easter faith.

The images used in this illustration, a roaring from heaven, storm, fire, come from the Old Testament, the Jewish Bible, and, like the indication of time 'at the feast of Pentecost', point to the Jewish tradition, according to which Moses received the laws on Mount Sinai from God, who descended with fire, thunder and storm. For Jews, the feast of Pentecost commemorates the Sinai event.

From some details of the sermon which Peter delivers next, biblical scholars have been able to infer that it is a later theological construction from a Gentile Christian perspective, and that the historical Peter could not have delivered it in this form to a Jewish audience (cf. 17/ 187f.). Moreover the linguistic miracle by which a crowd made up of the most varied peoples which had gathered there heard the apostles speaking 'each in his own tongue' indicates the legendary character of the Pentecost narrative.

But none of this could prevent the popes down to the present day from still regarding Pentecost as a real historical event in which the Christ who had ascended into heaven sent down the Holy Spirit upon his apostles and thus fitted them for their office as leaders and teachers of the church which he had founded, illuminated by the Spirit.

Popes and bishops, who regard themselves as the successors of Peter and the apostles, have exploited the advantage of such a special endowment with the gifts of the Holy Spirit. From now on the church could appeal to the Holy Spirit which illuminates, guides and hallows it in all its teachings and instructions.

Holy Spirit?

What is Holy Spirit? In the doctrine of the church the Holy Spirit is a mysterious third person who lives and is active within the 'Most Holy Trinity'. God communicates through the Holy Spirit.

In an understanding widespread among believers, the Holy Spirit is something like a divine prompter who whispers the truth in the ears of the biblical authors, the apostles and their successors, instils the right thoughts and words into them, preserves them from error, and instigates them to act rightly. In the popular consciousness, his role is best known in the virginal conception.

Originally the Holy Spirit was not a person but only a wind, a breath, the movement of air. Ancient Israel called him *'ruach Yahweh'*, the breath of God. 'Breath' was an image of life. When a person no longer breathed, life had departed. The 'breath' of God gave life. The 'spirit' was something which went out from God and communicated itself; it was something that could 'break out' in people. It was said of the prophets that they were 'seized by the spirit of God' when they stood up against injustice, hard-heartedness, idolatry and cultic piety and issued a call to redemption. It was expected that the coming Messiah would speak and act powerfully in the spirit of God.

Finally, when Jesus appeared, many people saw him as someone who had been seized by the spirit of God in this way and lived, spoke and acted completely in this spirit. And that was also their interpretation of him: Jesus is the Messiah, the one who has been anointed by the spirit. The spirit of the Lord rests upon him. God's spirit is at work in him. He brings God's spirit into the world.

His spirit continues to be active

Yet these people could experience something which can still be experienced today: Jesus could infect others with this spirit. The lives of those who are infected by the spirit and the character of Jesus can be completely changed. They can live in a more trusting and generous way, free from anxiety and with a greater readiness for love. 'But the fruit of the spirit is love, joy, peace, patience, kindness, gentleness, loyalty,' we read in Galatians.

The spirit of God which emanates from Jesus can also bring about greater freedom towards the teachings and instructions of religious institutions. The proclamation of the 'freedom of the children of God' which is made through the spirit was clearly directed against the religious establishment of Judaism and led to freedom. The spirit of God is the spirit of freedom. Anyone who is open to this spirit and has received it will gain an immediacy to Jesus and to God which largely avoids mediation and regimentation by the doctrines and instructions of the church authorities.

It is just like an inter-personal relationship: the more I am intimately associated and familiar with someone who has become important and normative for me, the less there is need of teachings and instructions from above downwards to persuade me to do what that person wants. The more I have taken over his or her spirit and character for myself, the more freely I can decide and act, independently of instructions. I am then acting 'in his or her spirit'.

In this sense, 'Holy Spirit' can become living and effective in those who commit their existence to Jesus and are open to his spirit. The receiving of the spirit is the communication of existence; not a cultic rite or a miraculous event which took place fifty days after the resurrection of Jesus and ten days after his ascension in Jerusalem.

Distributing the Holy Spirit

According to the traditional doctrine and practice of the church, the Spirit is handed on to the faithful by sacramental acts of worship. From the 'fullness of the Holy Spirit' which it has received and preserved and which it administers, the church distributes the Holy Spirit in hierarchically gradated doses to the faithful.

The normal portion for church people is already given at baptism; rather more at confirmation, so that believers 'come of age'. But they must not come too much of age, since then there would probably be problems of discipline. Therefore there are still considerable possibilities of increasing the scope and nature of possession of the Spirit. However, these are exclusively limited to the clergy, predominantly the senior clergy.

Those who receive the highest level of illumination by the Holy Spirit, like the Bishop of Rome, 'enjoy infallibility' (1/no.891).

Possession of truth by virtue of office?

I know a number of bishops in the German episcopate whose human qualities and theological competence are outstanding. What they say on the basis of these qualifications I take seriously and think hard about. But it is quite different when bishops, solely on the basis of their office, claim to be in possession of a better understanding of the faith.

According to a doctrine of the church which is emphasized time and again, the office of pope and bishops goes back to the apostles. They receive their office through the rite of laying on of hands at their consecration. The chain of bishops who lay on their hands thus create, symbolically and ritually, a link which extends back to the apostles. Indeed the chain reaches back still further, to Christ himself, who (although Jesus was a layman) as 'eternal high priest' is the real source of all episcopal and papal authority.

In the early church this was called 'apostolic succession'. Like the succession to the throne in the hereditary monarchies, here too not only office and charge, but also the necessary 'gifts', are inherited; however they are not inherited biologically, but in a sublimated spiritual way. Bishops at their consecration at the same time receive special gifts from the Holy Spirit which enable them to have higher knowledge of the divine truth, independently of whatever theological knowledge they have, and this makes them superior to all other believing Christians, even the most highly-qualified theologians. Simply by virtue of their office.

So they now have a superior knowledge of the will of God

and the divine revelation. Even in questions of moral behaviour they know significantly better than anyone else what is good or bad, what is pleasing or displeasing to God. This 'support of the Holy Spirit' is a tremendous thing!

One could almost be envious. As ordinary Christians we are often perplexed by all these questions, and despite all our mental efforts we cannot find any certain and final answers. We grope helplessly in the dark. And these people are given a higher insight into the truth, simply because a bishop consecrates them with the laying on of hands and thus elevates them to the 'magisterium'. Before this rite they were as stupid as we are.

I simply can't grasp that. But I've only been confirmed.

'Adherence' is enough!

In most of its doctrines the church points out that at this or that council the bishops, assembled there together with the pope, under the influence of the Holy Spirit, have decided thus and not otherwise. Fine! That establishes once and for all what is true and right and what is to be believed as the truth down the millennia. The decisions of the council thus achieve the status of infallible truths revealed by God.

The Catechism teaches: 'The infallibility promised to the church is also present in the body of bishops when, together with Peter's successor, they all exercise the supreme Magisterium . . . When the Church through her supreme Magisterium proposes a doctrine for belief as divinely revealed, and as the teaching of Christ, the definitions must be adhered to with the obedience of faith' (1/ no.891). So we finally stop asking about the truth of faith. Adherence is enough!

Nevertheless I have to investigate precisely what happened at the early councils in the fourth or fifth centuries. At that time the issues were the divinity of Jesus and its relation to his humanity. If I may simplify somewhat, with no intention of being blasphemous, the dispute was as to whether Jesus had to sneeze as God or as man, whether he reacted according to his human nature or his divine nature when he sat at table with women from among his followers, like Mary and Martha.

A few hundred men assembled at these councils, mostly bishops. Depending on the size of the area in which they were active, nowadays they would tend rather to be called area deans or archdeacons. As a rule they had little theological education and religious knowledge. Other qualifications were needed to become a bishop. At that time men qualified to be bishops more by administrative and political capacities, as indeed is still often the case today. High birth, preferably from the nobility, was a quite special qualification for the episcopate. Now they sat together and argued about the relationship between the humanity of Jesus and his divinity. They had to decide between the different doctrinal views which had been presented by keen-minded and eloquent spokesmen of the individual groups.

Anyone who has had occasion to take part regularly in conferences or meetings which make decisions and decide on guidelines will know all too well from experience how such majority decisions finally come about. As a rule, what is finally approved corresponds to the view of those who impose themselves most successfully.

Things will not have been different at the early christological councils.

So is what was decided at that time by around three hundred men at a council, in such a way, to be understood for centuries, for millennia, for the whole future history of humankind, as a final criterion which cannot be changed and about which no questions can be asked?

I cannot wholly suppress my doubts.

Illuminated by the Holy Spirit?

Anyone who has looked more closely at the history of the definition of dogmas in the great councils will also know with what highly questionable means decisions were often made; they will know about the bribery and the pressure of power politics.

The first dogma was proclaimed in 325 at the Council of Nicaea. Here Jesus, who had already become a divine Christ in Paul and in the Gospels, finally became God. The emperor Constantine, although not yet baptized, had convened the council and also financed it. With political pressure he forced through a formula according to which Jesus is 'of the same substance' (*homoousios*) as the Father and 'the divine substances are identical in both persons'. In the New Testament Jesus was still clearly subordinate to God. Now he himself became God, 'of one being with the Father'.

The decision which Constantine carried through was a political decision, not a theological one. It was not made in order to bring to light and safeguard a deeper truth about Jesus Christ. Here we have the 'unity of throne and altar' which is known well enough, the interplay of religious and political power.

For reasons of political power, Constantine had elevated Christianity to be the Roman state religion. As a religious appendage to political power, the church was to support the rule of the emperor and legitimate it by God. Had its founder been only a human being who had met with a wretched end on the cross as a blasphemer and rebel, of course the church could hardly have fulfilled this task. It could not have competed with the religions of Mithras, Apollo or Isis. Its founder *had to be* a god. Only a church appointed by God could sacralize the rule of the emperor and support it effectively. It was in the political interest of the emperor for Jesus to be of the same substance as God. So he ensured that this decision was made.

Nor did the church have any reason to be dissatisfied with the decision of Nicaea. So it has defended the divinity of Jesus tooth and nail down the centuries, and condemned anyone who dared to doubt this dogma. Only a Jesus who was a god could ensure the church a 'divine origin' and thus give it the status which it claimed.

Was it the spirit of Jesus, the spirit of God, which guided the church in Nicaea? Or was it the spirit of Caesar?

Ensuring orthodoxy

The process of the dogmatizing of the biblical faith by the church already began in the first Christian centuries. The experiences of God, meaning and truth which the Bible had articulated and handed down in the manifest ambiguity of mythical and figurative language were transformed into an abstract conceptuality which was concerned to draw precise, clear and sharp distinctions from other doctrinal views. Views which lay the other side of the line which it drew were thus quickly recognized as 'heresies' and excluded.

Whereas the Bible allows much scope and variety to interpretation, the dogmatic statements allow only a single interpretation, that of the church's magisterium. The divinely defined doctrine became the vehicle of an unchangeable truth. And only obedient acceptance of this definition, together with the historic language in which it was stated, guaranteed orthodoxy. The many doctrinal statements and definitions had to be related to one another and interconnected. Thus in the course of the centuries a comprehensive dogmatic system came into being which seemed intrinsically firm, harmonious and perfect.

The venture of faith was replaced by the granting of an officially authenticated 'certainty'. To dare is dangerous; certainty is safe. But the need for certainty was almost always rooted in anxiety. Jesus lived out his faith as loving and trusting commitment to God. This faith, to which Jesus called men and women, was turned into a faith which consisted in holding the doctrinal statements of the church's ministry to be true.

Belief in God was perverted into belief in an institution.

The price of 'certainty'

However, a high price had to be paid for the safeguarding of faith in a system of objectivized teachings. The dogmatic formulae are like empty shells which have lost their living content. Doctrinal formulae become empty formulae. They have no intrinsic life; they cannot hand on life. We can speak of God and the truth of faith only in language which is committed, in a language in which our own existence is brought into play.

The living truth, which once illuminated the minds and hearts of the people of the Bible; by which they were seized, cast down or raised up, overwhelmed and changed; this 'experience of God' escapes the objectifying langage of definition and administration. Linguistic formulae are defended; husks, words are handed on, but not faith.

As Martin Buber says, the eternal Thou can never be made an It, an object. If it is, it ceases to answer.

The most exciting topic of existence, the topic of God, becomes an extremely boring affair in the language of the magisterium, one in which hardly anyone is still interested. For hardly anyone can still recognize what it has to do with his or her life. The truth which faith means becomes remote from existence, experientially poor, formal and therefore incomprehensible.

Tombs of faith

The compilation of church doctrines in the Catechism seems to me to be like the catalogue of an ancient cemetery, a necropolis. All the tombs are neatly arranged by plots and rows, and numbered. Originally living experiences of God over thousands of years have been embalmed and laid in stone sarcophagi. Living experiences of trust in God died when they were transformed into 'revealed, unchangeable, eternal truths'. In the course of the centuries they have increasingly turned into unrecognizable mummies. Mummies do not preserve and arouse any living faith.

In the long run faith can only remain alive if time and again, in trust in God, it exposes itself to the painful journey through the darkness. Those who still keep clinging to the customary officially guaranteed ideas, to rigid formulae of tradition, out of anxiety about losing their certainties, those who are afraid of going through a constant 'transformation' and 'reshaping' of their faith, are only watching over tombs containing old bones.

Jesus does not lie in these tombs. I cannot find him there. He is alive. That is the Easter message: 'Why do you seek the living among the dead?'

Social agreements

From a sociological perspective the formulae of faith composed by the councils have the character of 'social agreements'. They are elements in a social mechanism by which a group distinguishes itself from others and thus guarantees its inner stability.

Those who recognize the formulae as valid truth thus join a group and subject themselves to its ordinances and hierarchical structures. Those who doubt them, ask questions about them or even deny them, are in danger of becoming isolated and outcast.

Here 'truth' is understood less in the cognitive sense of a correct understanding and grasp of a matter or a process. Here 'truth' has more a socializing function in the sense of an identification with the community. What is called 'truth' here did not come into being through a process of understanding and knowledge, but through social agreement. By adopting such a 'truth', the individual takes a place in the group and submits to its claim to be in possession of the truth. This leads to a stabilization of the composition of the group and a reinforcement of its power.

Rupert Riedl, who has done important research into the

biological foundations and evolutionary development of the capacity for knowledge, speaks of 'collective truths' which 'determine the not inconsiderable remnant of our convictions, in so far as these cannot be sufficiently based either on logic or on the assimilation of experiences . . . They are social agreements to reassure abiding uncertainty' (18/ 257).

Sociologically, the church, too, is a 'group'. The sociological regularities found in other groups, associations, clubs, businesses, parties or the like also occur in it. Its doctrinal formulae are less concerned with a 'truth' in the objective sense than with the stabilization of its composition through criteria for order which bring its members together and discipline them.

Thus the bitter and often hostile fights at the councils were not primarily about 'truth', but about the establishment of a unified teaching, in other words about uniformity, order, discipline, power. Other views had to be condemned as 'heresies' in order to establish the claim to be giving the only right teaching. The unswerving, rigid maintaining of such linguistic formulae down the centuries no longer conveys unconditionally timeless 'truth', but serves the continuity and survival of the institution in a highly effective way. The definition of the only right teaching became the touchstone of orthodoxy. It excluded from the faith all who doubted it.

Belief in God became belief in propositions.

Infallible?

The 1870 dogma of infallibility is also to be put in this context. It does not further discovery, deeper knowledge and the reliable preservation of truth. Other ways of discovering truth were more appropriate for that: the intellectual quest, inner truthfulness, the introduction of one's own experiences and those of others, critical examination, scientific research, intellectual controversy, argument, contradiction, the courage to make corrections, etc.

No, this dogma was not about the truth of the faith but about the submission of all bishops, all theologians and all the faithful to the authority of the pope. What is called 'truth' became a means of enforcing conformity. The possession of infallible truth, now officially confirmed by a council through the illumination of the Holy Spirit, guaranteed the papacy its position at the head of the church.

This also seemed to be advantageous for the church. An infallible pope at its head stabilized the institutional church, held it together, preserved it from being diverted into an uncontrollable variety of opinions and splitting apart into countless groups. The only true relationship to God and the only true understanding of his will became a matter of loyalty to the pope.

It could hardly be easier!

The dilemma of infallibility

The church paid a high price for the additional power and discipline which it gained through the dogma of infallibility. Too high a price! One day the church will be stifled by it. Through the infallibility of the magisterium the church has condemned itself for all time to an inability to learn. It cannot adopt and assimilate any new insights. Those who possess infallible truth can only instruct others; they cannot learn from them. One only gets closer to the truth if one keeps looking and correcting oneself. The magisterium cannot correct itself and concede error. It is doomed to infallibility.

Because the whole of reality is interconnected, doctrines which previously have been regarded as unconditionally true and right will be put in question by new insights in quite different spheres of reality. That is also true of the understanding of faith. Whereas in all other spheres of life the progress of knowledge opens up a new understanding which points towards the future and requires an examination of previous understandings, every pope is compelled to maintain and defend the doctrines of his predecessors, even if they are clearly non-sensical. The magisterium has become the prisoner of its own claim. The arrogance of the claim to infallibility continually leads the thought of the official church to become rigid and fossilized.

The gulf between the development of general human awareness and the instructions of the church's magisterium will grow wider and wider. Most people, including believers, have by now come to feel that the claim of a small group of males to inerrant possession of the truth is a slight on the capacity of everyone else to think and judge.

So most believers no longer take the teaching of papal letters and encyclicals seriously. At best it is tacitly ignored, even by priests and pastors. And for those among them who think and are well informed, the doctrines and instructions of the magisterium ask too much, and jeopardize their personal faith in the authority of the church government.

Many believers, laity and priests, prelates and professors, have developed strategies for undermining the system: outwardly they are loyal and obedient to the official line; inwardly they have their own special areas of thought, evaluation and conduct which 'are no concern of the bishop and the pope'.

'There are businesses which only exist and survive by ignoring what has been decided by the board of directors.' I heard that last night in a television interview with the well-known management consultant and Jesuit father Rupert Lay. He also pointed out explicitly that this also applied to the church.

I personally would not want to live with such a split in my faith.

Faith – obedience to an institution

The faith which Jesus lived out consisted in loving and trusting surrender to God, open obedience to God's will. It was a venture into uncertainty in the knowledge that it was supported by God. Jesus' faith was an encouragement to freedom, love and reconciliation.

The Roman magisterium has turned belief into a matter of obedience towards an institution. It attempts to subject the freedom and openness of questioning thought to the decrees of an authority. Belief in God which is ventured in trust has become a perfect system of doctrines and instructions which are to be accepted in faith.

It can hardly be a coincidence that state dictatorships have flourished in Catholic countries in particular. The uncritical obedience of believers expected by the magisterium and the effort to subject their thought and judgment to the instructions of the church authorities have produced a mentality among Catholics which encourages their submission in thought and consciousness to authoritarian governments.

Belief in Jesus brings freedom and encourages people to search and think for themselves. The belief that the magisterium requires of the faithful discourages questioning, free thought. It gives priority to the subjection of personal judgment and thought to the instructions of the authorities. This faith does not correspond to the spirit and the character of Jesus.

A firm support for faith?

Today at breakfast I read in a newspaper that many priests and laity of the Church of England are converting to the Catholic Church. Their reason is the admission of women to the priesthood. 'It is a spiritual betrayal of the things that we have been taught,' remarked a churchgoer. Richard Rutt, the former Bishop of Leicester, explained his conversion by saying that 'only Rome speaks with a clear voice on moral matters'.

A former colleague complained about '. . . all the Drewermanns and Ranke-Heinemanns who are destroying the faith with their criticism'. 'When will the bishops finally call a halt and put a stop to such people?,' he asked anxiously. 'The faithful need firm support in the church. They mustn't be deprived of that.' I was shocked at his negative judgment, and especially at the reasons he gave for it. He didn't ask whether these authors were in fact right or wrong. He simply asked about possible 'harmful consequences'. That made me suspicious and disturbed me.

Perhaps I am not sufficiently aware that most believers in the church are not looking primarily for 'truth' at all but for something quite different: a firm support and a stable orientation amidst the multiplicity of views and convictions; a home in a community of like-minded people which gives them security from the oppressive uncertainties at the periphery of life; and reliable teachings which have proved themselves over the centuries. And if one is really to be able to cling on to this support, it must be stable. It mustn't change. Any change is felt to be dangerous disintegration.

My experience is different: if one of my 'supports' collapses under the question of truth, then it simply becomes clear, often painfully so, that I have been clinging on to something which was not really a support at all. A 'support' which no longer provides support if one asks whether it is reliably grounded in the truth is no support, merely self-deception.

I would have been clinging on to some ideas that I had accepted at one time, but not to God.

Unwanted doubt

'And what, your Excellency, do you believe that I should believe?' That is a question which Friedrich Dürrenmatt put in an interview with the then Archbishop of Vienna, which I heard by chance on the car radio.

I remember that a few decades earlier the faithful had constantly been warned not to reflect too much on matters of faith. 'It is a form of arrogance to submit faith to the judgment of one's own reason,' I recall from my own religious instruction and from many lessons given by priests. 'One must simply believe what the church teaches, since God has entrusted the truth to it. The pope and the bishops tell us what we have to believe. Thinking on one's own leads to the sin of doubt in faith.' How true!

Those who obey this teaching will probably continue to be preserved from doubt. But does that really serve a deeper Christian faith? Most of the faith of believers stems from the human tendency to join groups and adopt their convictions. That certainly spares the brain from being burdened, but is it faith, faith as Jesus means it?

The disciplinary repression of doubt in the church does not serve the 'truth of faith'; it simply and solely serves to stabilize the official institutional church and its claim to the possession of the truth. Any doubt in one of its teachings is felt to be a threat to its monopoly of infallible truth. Where one believes that one already possesses the whole truth, doubt merely becomes a disruptive factor. Finally, God has entrusted the truth of faith to the pope and the bishops. Those who listen to them obediently and accept what they teach are freed not only from doubt but also from the burden of having to think for themselves.

What is true is already firm

Those who boast that they possess the inerrant truth will hardly understand the quest of a thought which gropes towards an understanding, which doubts, considers and ventures. For them there is no such thing as a searching approach to the truth which is concerned to understand it. For them it is finally certain for all time what the truth is.

Therefore again and again over the centuries the magisterium has kept feeling that new insights and new intellectual approaches are threatening and are a danger to faith. It has repudiated them, ignored them or even condemned them. All that is left for those who seek is obedient acceptance of the teaching which has already been formulated. Only if the search for God and truth leads to the result at which the church has already arrived is it approved and accepted.

Theologians who in their thinking, questioning and research arrive at results which diverge from the official line of church teaching must expect to be suspect, and to be disciplined with measures at a variety of levels. They can only avoid difficulties if they disguise their divergent understanding and do not give voice to it.

Guided by the spirit of Jesus?

A few days before Hitler's attack on Russia on 26 June 1941, which was to cost the lives of millions of people, the German bishops had a pastoral letter read from the pulpits. It said:

Dear members of the diocese,

In this grave hour for the Fatherland, which is having to wage a war of unparalleled extent on broad fronts, we admonish you to do your duty loyally, to endure bravely, to be ready for sacrifice, and to fight in the service of our people. We send a greeting of grateful love and deep blessing . . . As you fulfil the onerous duty of this time, in the harsh tribulations which will come upon you as a result of the war, may you be strengthened by the comforting certainty that you are doing God's holy will (4/ 569).

I don't want to criticize the bishops here for being blind and misled, as millions of others were at that time. But I regard the mere fact that such an appeal was composed by a group of bishops and read aloud in the churches on their orders as virtual proof of the falsity of the church's claim that the bishops are in a special way guided by the spirit of God and thus enabled to give instructions to the faithful.

Can bishops who have preached that Hitler's murderous war

against Russia was in accord with God's holy will still claim to give instructions to people in the name of God, to which believers 'are to adhere . . . with religious assent' (cf. 1/ no.892)?

Has a pope ever objected to this statement by the German bishops, which deeply contradicts the spirit of Jesus and the gospel, or even threatened to remove their permission to teach? Was Hitler, who had the lives of millions of people on his conscience and brought unspeakable suffering on men and women, ever excommunicated? On the contrary, in old photographs I see senior church dignitaries standing beside him and raising their hands in the Nazi salute.

As an 'ordinary believer', can one really believe that the pope and the bishops are guided and illuminated by the Spirit of Jesus more than other Christians? I have come to have considerable doubts about that!

I too had doubts

Spontaneous doubts often assail me quite vigorously and emotionally over many forms of expression of the church's faith which I am inclined to think more incidental and external.

I can remember an occasion when this doubt really erupted. It was a long time ago, at a ceremonial service in Cologne Cathedral. To the strains of the organ, and with ministers swinging incense, the cardinal, several bishops, numerous prelates, and a horde of priests entered the sanctuary in splendid vestments. 'The procession's coming,' whispered my Cologne friend to me, likening it to the carnival procession on the Monday before Lent.

I gladly confess that I could not entirely escape the magic spell of the liturgical drama which I witnessed for the next hour and a half. But time and again the question kept boring into my brain, 'What has all this to do with Jesus?' I kept hearing the words, 'Christ has determined, has instituted, is present among us, has cleansed us by his blood, rules over all, we his servants

. . .', but the Christ who functioned here as the supreme patron of the event bore little similarity to the Jesus of the Gospels in whom I believe.

What I saw, heard and experienced was more like the rituals of the priestly castes in Egyptian or Assyrian temples or the priestly chorus of Sarastro in Mozart's *Magic Flute*. But I couldn't discover Jesus in this scene. He played only an incidental role. What was performed here tended more to conceal him and make him unrecognizable. What was happening here was the pompous and self-centred presentation of itself by a priestly caste amidst a cloud of incense. It was a dazzling display with impressive magic. What had Jesus and his message been turned into?

And was what was happening here willed and appointed by Jesus? Was this what he had become man for, so that these people, personally chosen, commissioned and authorized by God, could perform such ceremonies and rites as worship of God in their pompous and imposing vestments? He must have been a comic God to enjoy such a 'service'!

What image of God is at work if one thinks that one can honour him in such a way? Seldom have I gone away from a service so full of doubt and discontent.

I keep feeling the same doubt when I see picture of the pope's appearances on television. I get very uneasy. I feel that the visual presentation of the church alone bars many people from access to Jesus, his person and his teaching, and indeed his church, and distorts it. Is what is depicted and performed here meant to be a visible expression of the revelation of an ultimately binding truth about God, the world and humankind?

Even now, I still keep having doubts.

Superstition tolerated

What I still do not understand is on the one hand the rigour with which the church's magisterium proceeds against indi-

vidual theologians who ask questions about such dubious
doctrines as infallibility or the virgin birth in a critical search for
truth, and on the other the tacit tolerance, even encouragement,
of the worst superstition in the veneration of Mary, the saints
and relics at pilgrimage places of in popular piety.

The church's doctrinal system remains incomprehensible,
alien and remote for most believers. Beneath this official system
of faith, popular piety has created its own world of faith, permeated by magical, superstitious and sentimental religious
elements which go back far into archaic religious feelings.

I have the impression that the preaching and pastoral letters
of the church, especially in regions with a traditional faith, are
not particularly interested in changing much. It seems that the
more the 'ordinary people' are bound in this way to the church,
its magical power and its priestly magic, the less they reflect on
the faith. Belief remains all the 'firmer', even if it is only superstition. Here the church does not seem to think it so important
and necessary to establish a claim to the truth.

Too much enlightenment could put the faith in danger.
Theology is only for theologians, not for the people. It is better
to direct and guide ignorant people. In this way, deeper insight
into the mysteries of faith continues to be reserved for the
priests. That preserves their superiority to the flock and guarantees that the ordinary believers will look up with respect to their
priestly masters.

The fellowship of believers

Last night, quite late, I once again read through what I had just
written. As I did, I became aware that here I have used the word
'church' one-sidedly in the sense of 'church hierarchy' and
'official church'.

When I wrote 'church', I almost always had in mind only that
institution which sets itself apart from the other believers, the
people of the church, with the claim that it has been authorized

by Christ in a special way to lead them and has been equipped with special gifts by the Holy Spirit to do this. By 'church' I meant that church which is admirably personified in the figure of the pope.

But is that the real church? For me the church is first of all the community of all believers, the community which has the person of Jesus at its centre. The church is the whole people of God, the many, many millions of people, not just Catholics, who believe in Jesus Christ and his God. The spirit of Jesus continues to live and work in them. In all modesty I include myself in this church. I dare to do so because I believe in Jesus Christ. The church helps me to remain bound to Jesus.

The pope and bishop also belong to it as believers. They have an important service to perform in the church, but like other believers – despite faith and good will – they remain erring and mistaken human beings, with limited personal and historically-conditioned insight into the truth, even in matters of faith and morals. Their claim to be enlightened and guided by the Holy Spirit in a special way simply on the basis of their office, and as a result to have deeper and more correct insight into the truth and to know better than other believers what is right or wrong, good or reprehensible, raises the question whether in so doing they can rightly appeal to Jesus Christ and his Holy Spirit.

13

The mysterious rose

Mary

All my life as a believer I have always been in two minds about
Marian piety. While I was still working for the church I was
quite perplexed at the veneration of Mary customary in the
church and above all at the dogmas about Mary.

I have never been able to find a meaningful place for the
church's teaching about Mary in my faith. What I have
observed, perceived, heard, whether among so-called 'ordinary
people' or from spiritual dignitaries at every level of the hierarchy, and what I have read in the church literature, has made
me, if anything, far more sceptical.

Openness to an ultimate reality called God, yes! A deep personal commitment to the person and teaching of Jesus, yes!
And, following from that, solidarity with the community of
those who believe in Christ, called the church, yes! But not the
cult of Mary and her immaculate, sinless conception; Mary who
before during and after the birth of Jesus remained virgin; Mary
who after her death was taken up into heaven, body and soul,
where she is the mediatrix of all graces and intercedes with her
Son, so that he hears our prayers; Mary who occasionally
appears on earth to young girls, sends messages to humankind
and bestows springs of miracle-working saving power.

For me all these have always been incredible theological constructions which have disturbed my Christian faith rather than
supporting it. For me they are on the verge of superstition, and
they often cross the line. I have never been able to accept this
form of expression of the Christian faith.

No, that's not quite true. Now I remember. I had been sick; not dangerously ill, but quite life-threatening. At that time in fact I once prayed before an image of Mary in a pilgrimage church and asked for healing. Was this an atavistic lapse into magical and mythical primal forms of religion in a state of existential threat and a diminished capacity for rational thinking? Or what? At all events, here I fell existentially into a primal form of human behaviour which has been, and still is, found in all religions of this earth at all periods of history.

Does the existential truth about the cult of Mary perhaps lie beyond all the incredible Marian dogmas of the church, and beyond all distorting practices of piety, beyond the kitsch and the art, beyond the 'typically Catholic', beyond the universally Christian, beyond belief and unbelief, at a much deeper level of human existence? Does this 'truth' perhaps come from the depths of the human soul itself?

While remaining critical, here I want to try to find a way through all the obstacles presented by the church's cult of Mary to a deeper level, at which it is possible to recognize, or at least to have an inkling of, a more acceptable meaning for the veneration of Mary.

The great-great-great-great grandmother

By the Danube, where the rich wine-producing area of Wachau begins, between the apricot trees and the vine-clad slopes, there is a place which is small but has a well-known name, Willendorf. It owes its reputation to a small stone figure, only a few centimetres large, which was found at the beginning of our century when a railway was being built there: the famous Venus of Willendorf.

Her breasts, stomach and bottom are disproportionately large, whereas her head, face and hands are only hinted at. The small cult figure of the mother deity, an archaic fertility goddess dating back to the Stone Age people who settled in the Danube valley around twenty-five thousand years ago, can now be admired in the Natural History Museum in Vienna.

However, it is worth making a detour into the village of Willendorf from the road along the Danube, since at the place where it was discovered there is an enlarged copy of this Venus. When I take friends there I always tell them, 'This is the great-great-great-great grandmother of blessed Mary'. In the inn 'By the Venus', near the place where the little statuette was found, over a snack and a glass of admirably dry white wine I later tell them what I mean.

The Great Mother

In fact, female fertility goddesses stand at the obscure beginnings of the countless generations of deities who have been venerated, worshipped and invoked by human beings. Life originates and emerges from the woman's womb: in primeval times the survival of the family, the clan and the people depended on women's fertility. The natural fertility of the woman found its mythical sacralization in the fertility and mother deities.

So mother deities play a major role in the religions of the early period alongside deities who are thought of as male. In archaic religions their cult may even have been the dominant one. The Magna Mater, the Great Mother, is the one who graciously preserves, who bestows life in childbearing, who gives and protects. She is like the fertile 'mother earth' which brings food for human beings from its dark womb. So at a very early stage fertility deities and vegetation deities were combined in the figure of the Magna Mater.

In primeval human times, the gathering and harvesting of the fruits of the earth was women's work, while the men went out hunting. Women 'knew' the 'mystery' of fertility, the mystery of their bodies and of the earth. And this was a sacral and religious mystery, because it embraced the origin of life, its nourishment and its death, and also its rebirth. Over millennia, for early humankind it was 'mother earth' which all by itself bore life-sustaining fruits from its bosom, by means of a 'partheno-genesis', a virgin birth (cf. 8/ 47f.)

Perhaps the earliest beginnings of the religious notions of a virgin mother deity which later emerge in numerous ancient myths and found their Christian expression in the figure of the virgin mother Mary must be sought here.

An image from pagan myths

The notion of virgin motherhood in fact appears in many religions, quite independently. Many myths tell how sons of god, redeemers and saviours sent by God, godlike kings, heroes and other significant people were born from the union of a god with a virgin.

Buddha was already born from the virgin mother Maya around 500 BCE. She had conceived through a white elephant. Hera, the consort of the Greek Zeus, was originally a universal fertility goddess. According to Mircea Eliade, her union with the god Zeus is 'the typical image of union between a fertilizing storm God and the earth mother' (8/ 257). However, she gave birth to her son Hephaestus all by herself, without a husband.

Artemis, the great goddess of Ephesus, was a virgin, indeed a 'perpetual virgin' (8/ 258). At the same time she was venerated as a goddess of fertility and a mother goddess, as is indicated by the cultic figures with many breasts which have been found. Pallas Athene, who sprang from the forehead of Zeus, was also a virgin.

Perseus and Heracles, the sons of gods, were fathered by a god in the womb of a virgin. It is also reported of Plato, Alexander the Great and the Roman Emperor Augustus that they emerged from the union of a god with a virgin. In Persia, Zarathustra was worshipped as the son of a virgin. In celebrat-ing the birth of the sun-god Mithras in the night of 25

December, the date of present-day Christian Christmas, the priests of Mithras proclaimed: 'The Virgin has given birth. Light is coming.'

The Egyptian Pharaoh, who was regarded as an incarnation of the deity, and from whom 'salvation and life' emanated for the people, was begotten by Amon-Re, the god of wind and spirit, in the virgin queen, by breathing on her. Wind, breath and spirit are almost synonymous in the language of myth. The parallels to the depiction of the conception of Jesus are very striking here.

Although the figure of the virgin mother goddess is depicted in various ways in the individual religions, something more, deeper and different is meant by the image of the virgin than mere physical and biological integrity, an intact hymen, or 'purity' understood in moral terms.

As can easily be demonstrated from the history of religion, the notion of a virgin mother from whose womb a divine bringer of salvation emerges is not unique to the Christian religion, nor is it a Christian invention. It extends back for many millennia beyond the New Testament, far into the earliest period of the human race. The image of the virgin mother is one of the archetypes of the religious consciousness and is deeply rooted in the human soul. Mary is not the first virgin mother. Not only the archaic fertility deities but also the Hellenistic virgin goddesses are certainly among her ancestors. The similarities are unmistakable.

An important difference

However, despite all the similarities, there is an important difference between the virgin mother Mary and her pagan ancestors. Christian theologians keep stressing these.

In the biblical account , no God has sexual intercourse with a human virgin. The biblical God is not the partner of Mary, who fathers her child, not even in the form of the Holy Spirit.

The notion of a *hieros gamos*, a sacred marriage between a god and an earthly virgin, was completely alien to Jewish religious thought. Indeed, it was contrary to it, and incompatible with its image of God.

For the notion of God in the Old Testament developed in the centuries-long battle of Israel against the fertility religions of its environment. Israel's God was not a divinized power of nature. Nature, including sexuality and fertility, was desacralized in Jewish religion. Nature was not divine; sexuality and fertility were not divine powers. Only the one God, the Wholly Other, was divine. He was Lord of nature, not part of it.

The image of a virgin who brings a divinely-begotten divine saviour into the world has no adequate background in the Old Testament, Jesus' Bible. Nor does a virgin birth of the Messiah play a role in the Jewish expectation of salvation. Nowadays almost all Christian exegetes concede that the notion of a virgin birth in fact derives from myths of gods outside the Bible.

The virgin birth – a legend?

The Hellenistic myths of sons of virgins fathered by gods was widespread in the religious and geographical environment of the early Christians at the time the New Testament was composed. This model and imagery which already existed in the surrounding world was taken up and transformed in order to express and provide a basis for post-Easter belief in Jesus the Son of God, especially in the Gentile Christian communities.

The stories of the virgin birth of Jesus that we hear at Christmas are therefore not depictions of miraculous historical events which took place at the beginning of Jesus' life. They are modes of expression close to myths, which served to support, depict and illustrate a belief that had already existed for decades, that Jesus is the Messiah. So theologians call them 'aetiological legends', i.e. legends which after the event provide a 'cause' (Greek *aitia*); in this case of the messiahship of Jesus.

Expert theologians now take this understanding of the stories
of the birth of Jesus for granted in their work. Only the pope in
Rome still seems stubbornly to resist this insight of his theologians, and argues as though the miraculous events at the birth
of Jesus really took place as they are described. Is he worried
about his cult of Mary?

Born of a woman

In the earlier writings of the New Testament there is still appar-
ently no awareness of a virgin birth of Jesus. Paul, who in his
letters already depicts Jesus as an eternal son of God come down
from heaven in divine splendour, says nothing about a miraculous birth. He simply says 'born of a woman' (Gal.4.4). Nor do
we read at any point in other writings in the New Testament,
either in Mark and John or in Acts or the apostolic letters, that
Jesus was born of a virgin. At no point in the Gospels does Jesus
refer to his miraculous birth from a virgin.

The virgin birth is mentioned only right at the periphery of
the New Testament, in Matthew and Luke. They give their
Gospels 'a story of Jesus' childhood' in which mention is made
of a virgin birth, almost as a prelude. The infancy narratives
appear in these Gospels as an element which did not originally
belong, which was added later and is therefore hard to reconcile
with what is related in them. They in fact come from a later
time.

At first the birth of Jesus probably played no role in the faith
and proclamation of the primitive church.

Interwoven with images from the Old Testament

According to many exegetes there is reason to suppose that the
birth legends came into being in pagan Christian communities,
since the Hellenistic myths of sons of god, begotten by gods and

fathered by virgins, were influential there, and continued to be. The legend of the birth of the Messiah from a virgin suited the Hellenistic environment and corresponded to its notions.

For Christians who came from the Jewish tradition, however, it was more difficult to believe in the birth of the Messiah from a virgin. There were no virgin births in the world of Jewish faith. Matthew and Luke therefore had to insert the pagan theme of the 'virgin birth', which is alien to Jewish thought, into the world of Jewish ideas. And they did this by interweaving it with texts and narratives from the Jewish Bible, the Old Testament.

For example, Mary was put in the context of great female figures of the Old Testament who were made fertile by divine intervention. Their sayings, like other sayings from the Old Testament, were now put into her mouth. So the famous Magnificat, the song of praise with which Mary responds to the message of the angel, is modelled almost word for word on a song of praise from the Old Testament books of Samuel, in which Hannah, the mother of Samuel, who had long remained barren, thanks God for the birth of her son (cf. Luke 1.47ff. with I Sam.2.1-10). Moreover this Magnificat is packed with quotations from the Old Testament. The historical Mary, who probably could neither read nor write, could never have spoken it. This composition, made up of quotations from the Old Testament, was created only later, in Jewish Christian communities. Exegetes call it a community formation.

The angel's words, 'Blessed are you among women', also come from the Old Testament (cf. 23/63f.). With these words an angel originally praises a woman called Jael who cruelly kills the enemy general Sisera when he seeks help in her tent in his flight: 'Most blessed of women be Jael. She put her hand to the tent peg, and her right hand to the workmen's mallet. She struck Sisera a blow, she crushed his head, she shattered and pierced his temple' (Judg.5.24f.). A most macabre origin for praise of Mary!

'A virgin will bear a child'

There are no virgins who give birth in Jewish religion. Nevertheless, Matthew looks for one in the Old Testament, and actually finds her, in the prophet Isaiah. This book contains a sentence which nowadays is usually translated in Catholic Bibles with the words, 'Behold, a virgin will conceive and bear a son' (Isa.7.14).

But that is not what the original Hebrew Bible says. In it we do not have 'virgin', but 'young woman' (Hebrew *alma*). And even at that time it was known that a young woman was not necessarily a virgin. In the Greek translation of the Hebrew Bible, the so-called Septuagint, *alma* was later translated with the Greek word *parthenos*, which means virgin. This 'young woman', who was to have a child in a quite normal way, became a 'virgin', thought of in Hellenistic terms (cf.15/55).

Nor did these words promise through the forecast of a prophet – as church people are always told – a redeemer who was Son of God and would be born of a virgin almost seven hundred and fifty years later. Matthew has torn them from their original context. In it there is no mention of a miraculous event of the distant future, but of a very present threat to Israel by its enemies, the Assyrians. Isaiah's encouragement to king Ahaz is that before the boy grows up, 'the land of whose kings of whom you are in dread will be desolate' (Isa.7.16).

In Matthew, the misunderstanding of the words of the prophet based on an incorrect translation become a 'scriptural proof' of the virgin birth of Jesus: 'All this came to pass that what was spoken by the Lord through the prophets might be fulfilled.' Thus by means of a scriptural quotation from the Old Testament, a pagan myth became a historical miracle. And understood in this way, it later also came to be fixed in dogma. The young Jewish woman Miriam, who gave birth to Jesus, thus became the perpetually pure and immaculate virgin Mary.

A *biological miracle?*

In the church tradition, the virginal conception and birth of Jesus are understood in a thoroughly physical and biological way: Mary miraculously became pregnant without having had intercourse with a man, and also remained virgin in and after the birth of Jesus. That is what the church still teaches today.

In the period during which this tradition was developing, in antiquity and in the Middle Ages, people did not have any great difficulty in imagining that God had made the womb of the virgin Mary fruitful through a miracle. At that time knowledge of how new life came into being was still very inaccurate. It was not yet known that a female ovum had to be fertilized by a male sperm. The female ovum was only discovered in the early nineteenth century. In antiquity, the woman's womb was usually regarded simply as an empty container in which the man's seed was placed in order to mature to fruit there.

Because so little was known about the processes of pregnancy and birth, conception and birth, like sickness and death, always verged on the miraculous. On several occasions the Bible reports about barren women who have unexpectedly become pregnant through a miraculous intervention by God. Why should God not also have made Mary pregnant through a miracle?

However, our present knowledge of ova and sperms, of genes and chromosomes, of the biological processes in the procreation and development of a child in the womb, makes it very difficult for us to follow the traditional teaching in the customary way, as a biological statement about a virginal conception of Jesus.

Indeed, for many people today a doctrine of the virgin birth understood in biological and miraculous terms has become a serious obstacle to faith. For more and more people this doctrine is a reason for dismissing the whole of Christian faith as an incredible fairy tale, and for parting company with it. Many believing Catholics in the church also no longer accept the traditional doctrine in this way. I know from many personal conversations with priests and well-known theologians that they too see and interpret the virgin birth differently from the magisterium. And I too must personally confess that I can no longer believe in the doctrine of the virgin birth of Jesus in this biological miraculous sense, as it is still put forward, at least officially, by the pope and the bishops.

The truth lies deeper

Although I personally can no longer follow the magisterium's understanding of the virginal conception in the traditional sense, I usually deliberately join in saying the phrase 'born of the Virgin Mary' in the creed at mass. That is because I believe that in this formula, behind the superficially miraculous, a deeper truth lies hidden, a truth to which I can still open myself even now.

Most of the difficulties with the virgin birth disappear almost automatically when I read the narratives of the birth of Jesus, not as an account of facts, but as a deep and beautiful poetic picture which has been painted against a multi-dimensional background. This background is formed by Hellenistic myths and Old Testament accounts, while in the foreground is belief in Jesus Christ. From a literary perspective the birth story is a legend, and a legend must be read and understood differently from a factual account. A legend too can contain truth.

The 'truth' of the biblical birth legend certainly does not lie in the miraculous events depicted there. These are merely a way of depicting something quite different and far more important. They seek to proclaim to Jews and Gentiles the belief that Jesus is the expected Messiah. The 'truth' of the birth legends lies there. They do not seek to give information about mysterious processes in Mary's body which led to the birth of Jesus. They are not documentation of a gynaecological condition.

Decades before the Christmas stories came into being, there
was a belief in Jewish and Gentile Christian communities that
Jesus was Son of God, i.e. the Messiah, the Christ. This faith
appealed to the Easter experience, not to birth from a virgin.
The narrative of the virgin birth is a later legendary development and illustration of a faith which was already present
and being lived out. The credal formula 'born of the virgin
Mary' is not a statement about Mary but a statement about
Jesus, who has communicated God to humankind in a completely new way.

Is it really absolutely necessary for the magisterium, out of
loyalty to the tradition, to hold fast to an understanding of the
virgin birth which rests on an ancient belief in miracles and a
defective knowledge of the peculiarity of biblical terminology?
Doesn't loyalty to the tradition rather obligate the pope and
bishops once again to show the real truth that is hidden in this
legendary form of description, by conceding that the truth does
not lie in the miraculous character of the legendary mode of
description but in what this legend seeks to proclaim, belief in
Jesus Christ?

That would open up an understanding of the virgin birth of
Jesus which would make it possible even for thinking people to
believe today.

Purity?

To those who venerate Mary most piously, 'purity' has become
one of the most important characteristics of the virgin mother.
She is not only the 'purest virgin' but even the 'most pure of all
virgins'. Here 'purity' and 'intactness' are celebrated in ever new
variations.

Purity – what does that really mean? If someone is said to be
pure, it indicates a high regard for his or her humanity. It points
to a purity of personal disposition and motivation. But such
'purity' certainly has nothing to do with an intactness under-

stood in physical and sexual terms, and is not to be identified with this.

The fact that a woman has given birth to five or even ten children does not make her unclean. One could speak of her in the same words as those said of Mary in the Christmas hymn: 'She has born a child, yet remains a pure maiden.' To assert otherwise would be a humiliating insult to all mothers. No woman is made unclean by the birth of a child.

Nor does 'purity' have anything to do with sexual continence or prudery. A woman who gives herself sensually and with great pleasure to her beloved husband, and in so doing imaginatively enjoys her own sexuality, need not lose anything of the purity of her love and her heart in so doing. To assert otherwise would be a slight on the love between man and woman which is part of creation.

The words 'purity' and 'virginity' symbolically indicate a new beginning. They point to the beginning of a new life, a new hope. They point to the opportunity of a completely new beginning which is not yet burdened by the past. They stand for something which is not yet corrupted by baseness, banality and crudeness.

They open up a new horizon of life and point to a completely new possibility of living. Virginity is always also a hopeful expectation of fulfilment to come. Virginity stands for openness: openness to the new, the coming, the greater, the better. Virginity stands for something which has not yet become rigid, hardened and encrusted in the human soul.

When the language of faith speaks of the 'pure virginity' of Mary, it means none other than the beginning of a completely new possibility of living truthfully, lovingly and near to God; a possibility which has been disclosed to humankind by Jesus, her Son.

Jesus calls those blessed who are 'pure in heart'. But when the 'purity' of the Virgin Mary is celebrated in the language of the church, the reference is not to the purity of which Jesus speaks. In customary church terminology – and I must state this harshly

– in a crudely primitive way what it in fact means is that, in an almost exclusive physical understanding, the sexual parts of a woman have not been touched by a man's hand, have not been 'damaged' by man's force, and have not been 'stained' by a man's seed.

Such an understanding of 'purity' cannot appeal to Jesus, nor to divine revelation; rather, it indicates an archaic, musty, masculine way of thinking which is still widespread today, particularly in the Romance and Iberian countries of the Mediterranean and South America. There, but not only there, the 'pure, intact maiden' whom no other man has possessed is still the preferred object of male wishes.

Virginity – regarded in phylogenetic terms

The roots of such a preference for a 'pure, intact virgin' may lie in the biological ancestry of humankind. They are grounded in a control of behaviour which extends back far before the Stone Age, into archaic early forms of human propagation.

Evolutionary behavioural research explains this with reference to the so-called 'selfish gene'. Any male being – and this is already the case with animals – is driven by innate genetic behavioural control to reproduce his own gene as successfully as possible in the face of the genes of rival species. The male therefore wants to be certain that no other male has already established his gene in the womb of his woman. And the man can only be sure of this if the woman is an 'intact, pure virgin'. Therefore in some cultures even today, young women must submit to an inspection of their physical virginity before marriage.

This archaic biological and sexual control of behaviour, which has been acquired phylogenetically, comes into play in the background of the religious veneration of the 'intact, pure virgin' Mary, even in its most spiritual form. This gives 'intact virginity' a quite special fascination. This fascination has been genetically stored in the brain for tens of thousands of years and influences thought, evaluation and behaviour, even if in specific instances individuals have no inkling of it and believe that they are thinking and acting for 'purely religious' reasons.

The cult of Mary and celibacy

Religiously motivated men and women who want to be completely free for service of God's cause and their fellow human beings, and therefore renounce the physical fulfilment of their sexuality in marriage and family, find a possibility of identifying with the figure of the intact virgin Mary, depicted in a heightened form. The veneration of Mary who remained virgin 'before, during and after giving birth' can give them strength for their renunciation and their service. I gladly recognize such a religious motivation in many clergy, male and female religious, priests and bishops, and it is to be respected greatly.

But is that all that leads those, particularly men, who live a celibate life to such an ardent veneration of Mary? My question now is not theological, but psychological. (The theological justification is usually simply a rationalization of drives from the depths of the human soul which is usually given only after the event.) My question is about the motivations arising from the psyche which come from a deeper level of the unconscious, below conscious thought.

It is hard to overlook a connection between celibacy and the cult of Mary. It is no coincidence that veneration of Mary has faded into the background in the Protestant church, which draws its faith from the same biblical sources. Nor has any comparable cult been able to develop around the figure of a 'pure virgin' in Judaism and Islam.

The Catholic picture of Mary has been painted predominantly by celibate males. The figure of Mary has been exalted high above all natural feminine features, in order to 'purify' her of all that gives women a seductive power over men which can drag them down into the 'abasement of sin'. A woman who has been 'purified' in this way can no longer become dangerous. She can be approached without anxiety. She only draws men 'upwards'.

By way of compensation, repressed male sexuality creates the image of the ever pure woman to whom one can devote oneself in ardent veneration, without becoming 'unclean'. Above all for clergy living a celibate life, the cult of Mary becomes an anchor to which they can attach themselves in order not to be torn away by the surging flood of natural male longings.

When one listens to the pope and some other clergy talking, it almost seems as if the message of Jesus turned on nothing but 'virginal' purity, human sexual behaviour. But Jesus did not say a word about this. It is not the teaching of Jesus that stands at the beginning of the clerical ideology of purity, but Gnostic dualistic pagan philosophy.

When I consider the stylization of Mary as the 'ever pure' virgin from a psychological perspective, I can understand the sometimes almost painful gestures of homage from her clerical admirers at all levels of the church hierarchy. The lyricism of the celibate praise of Mary hardly differs in its devoted inwardness from subtle erotic poetry. It uses the same language and the same imagery.

The mother of mothers

But what leads women, quite normal women with a husband and children, to have a devotion to Mary which is different, but no less ardent?

I have often talked with women about their veneration for Mary and asked them the reason. The many different reasons they give for their Marian piety almost always amount to this: 'She is a mother like me. She understands me. She is a woman. I can say anything to her.'

These are certainly not theological answers, but they are answers from the heart, answers from the depth of the soul on which the picture of the helping and understanding mother is engraved. It is not just that individual experiences and reminiscences from their own childhoods have drawn this picture in their souls; the picture is older and more universal. It is an image which has impressed itself as an archetype on the subconscious in a long human history.

The image of the helpful and understanding mother keeps rising from the depths of the soul, particularly in times of need and oppression. In the Christian tradition, by way of projection it combines itself with the figure of the mother of Jesus, who is transfigured and elevated. Thus for countless Christian believers Miriam of Nazareth, the simple Jewish housewife and mother, becomes a new Great Mother, a Christian Magna Mater.

Mary stands for motherhood *par excellence*. She acquired such great significance, particularly in popular piety, because her figure corresponded precisely to the Magna Mater. In the Christian sphere she entered into the heritage of the old mother deities and thus really became a 'comforter of the troubled', a 'place of refuge', a 'mother of perpetual help'.

As I write this I keep thinking of my own mother, who made a pilgrimage to Kevelaer every year and ardently prayed to Mary.

The Madonna

I remember the great Hindu temple in New Delhi. Before the figure of a female deity with a child in her arms, Indian women were lighting candles and prostrating themselves in prayer. I was deeply impressed by the similarity of this picture to the pictures of Madonnas which I knew from the Catholic churches at home. Only the Indian garments distinguished this maternal deity from the figures of Mary in our churches. Everything else was the same.

And probably the same thing is happening both here and there; it is the same universal human action which flows from the depths of the human heart; here among us and there among the Hindus. No specifically Christian or even Catholic theme is reflected here in the figure of the Madonna, the mother with the child exalted to sanctity. It is a fundamental theme of all humankind: the mother and the child.

Alongside the Christian Madonna stand numerous maternal deities from other religions who reflect the elementary human experiences of the mother- child relationship in the splendour of divine motherhood in the same way as Mary. So we keep finding the image of the Madonna in many variants in the religious myths of humankind. The Egyptian Isis with her divine son Horus was also depicted as a Madonna with child.

What a good thing that there's Mary!

The human soul longs for the security of a mother. All mother deities have been born from this longing of the heart. The female element, including the feminine in males, has a drive towards reflecting itself personally against the background of the divine, just like the male. The great goddesses of the ancient world performed this service and in their sanctuaries attracted the longing of countless people.

The monotheistic religions, Judaism, Christianity and Islam, have suppressed the female deities in their spheres of existence. The God of these religions is male. He is depicted by a male image, and he tolerates no other divinity beside him. But the expulsion of the pagan goddesses has torn a gap in the human soul and left it open. And the Christian cult of Mary has been able to take up a new home in this gap. In this gap Mary has grown up to become a new Great Mother.

Mary is the only feminine being who occupies a prominent place within a religion stamped by male thought. In the Catholic countries of the Mediterranean and South America, and also in Poland and Ireland, she has often been able to displace Jesus, her Son, and even God himself from the centre of piety. Mary has become powerful. Granted, official church theology keeps emphasizing that Mary is not a goddess, but in practical piety, from the 'ordinary little mother' to the pope, the cult of Mary is hardly different from that of a female deity.

No comparable development of a cult with a feminine stamp has taken place in Islam and Judaism. Is that to their advantage? Perhaps Christianity has also gained some advantages over these religions through its veneration of Mary. What I mean is that Christianity can be gentler, warmer, more inward, more tender, more poetic, more friendly, more feminine, more reconciling, more human. (Perhaps I may be also mistaken here, however, since the image of Mary was also carried before murdering, burning and pillaging armies, like that of a goddess of war.)

However, countless people have entrusted the distresses and anxieties of their lives to the virgin mother Mary and in so doing have found consolation, strength and understanding. She has really become a 'comforter of the disturbed'. Countless people have looked for help and healing in her and have found it in some way.

The cult of Mary reduces and tones down at least the one-sided male patriarchal stamp of the monotheistic religions. Therefore I can take up the title of a well-known German television series and say, 'What a good thing there's Mary!'.

Taken up into heaven

The little Galilean girl Miriam, called Mary in Latin, has in fact 'ascended into heaven', but in a different sense from that understood by the dogma of 1950.

Mary has come to occupy the place once occupied by the great goddesses. She inhabits the spheres in which they once lived. She sits on the throne from which they once ruled. She has been given the garments they once wore. Her neck has been adorned with the jewellery which once adorned theirs. The ordinary wife of a craftsman, the housewife and mother, has become a 'queen of heaven'.

The Egyptian goddess Isis was already called Queen of Heaven, Sancta Regina, Queen of the Sea, Immaculate, Redeemer, Giver of Grace, Helping Mother. She was even called God-bearer and Mother of God. Isis, too, was a virgin when she bore her son Horus. The blue cloak decorated with stars which Mary still wears today comes from Isis's wardrobe (cf. 7/ 399f.). And the crescent with the star, under her feet, which we see in many depictions of Mary, originally comes from the cult of Isis, which in Ephesus was fused with that of the fertility goddess Artemis and the moon goddess Cybele.

The cult of Isis was still widespread in the Roman empire in the first Christian centuries. Christianity only gradually detached itself from the religion of Isis. In the process not only was the title of Isis transferred to Mary but the cult places of Isis also became sanctuaries of Mary. The well-known Roman church Maria Supra Minerva stands on the foundations of a temple of Isis.

Numerous people in the Mediterranean made pilgrimages at that time to Ephesus, to an image of the fertility goddess Artemis which performed miracles. According to legend, it had fallen from heaven. Will not something similar have been said of an image of Mary in some Christian places of pilgrimage? It was Isis and Artemis who in 431 rose at the Council of Ephesus in a new form, that of the Christian Mary. She had simply been baptized.

Even the old fertility goddess lives on in Mary. When my wife had still not become pregnant after almost a year of marriage, and was worrying that she might never have a child, my mother urged her to go with her to Kevelaer and pray to Mary there. The two women went. And nine months later our first child was born. Now tell them that Mary did not help!

In Ohlsdorf in Upper Austria, near the Traunsee, a picture of the pregnant Mary adorns the high altar. Many women hoping to become mothers, so far in vain, make long pilgrimages there every year seeking help from this picture. Artemis lives on.

Marianism and papalism

We know little of the historical Mary. We do not know the names of her parents, we do not know where and when she was born, nor even when and where she died. Most of what is related about her life has come from pious fantasy. She plays only a subsidiary role in the New Testament. She is a marginal figure. It is impossible to discover whether she occupied a particularly elevated position in the earliest community during her lifetime. Nor does she seem to have understood much of what her son said and did. Despite being instructed by an angel at the beginning of her pregnancy, she regarded later events around Jesus with incomprehension. Indeed, the relationship between Jesus and Mary even seems to have been a tense one.

From a theological perspective, too, the doctrine of the virgin Mary is not a central content of Christian faith. It has a low place within the so-called 'hierarchy of truths'. In the first Christian centuries there was no marked veneration of the mother of Jesus. This came into being in the East between the third and fifth centuries and became more strongly established in the Western Church during the Middle Ages.

Meanwhile Mary has grown from having a subsidiary role in church piety to having almost a main role, at least in the papal Catholic form of Christian faith.

Since the Counter-Reformation, the cult of Mary has become a distinguishing characteristic of Catholic 'orthodoxy'. Marian piety has become the odour of Catholicism. Anyone who has reservations about the church's teaching about Mary, anyone who is not loyal to the magisterium in sharing belief in the Marian dogmas and can only accept with reservations the cult of Mary in its often superstitious forms, is not a 'full believer'. Such a person is almost heretical. By contrast, a zealous Marian piety safeguards careers in the church hierarchy and is regarded as an important criterion of selection in the nomination of bishops.

The reason for the papal encouragement of the cult of Mary

in its many forms – from the proclamation of Marian dogmas to the toleration of the worst superstition at Marian pilgrimage places – is less a matter of theology than of power politics. The Catholic cult of Mary serves to mark Catholicism off from Protestantism and to reinforce the papacy. In Mary the Roman church glorifies itself.

Marianism and papalism encourage each other.

The two Marys

The historical Mary was probably born in Nazareth, though we do not know precisely, but the cultic Mary, the 'Mary of faith', was born in Ephesus, almost four hundred and fifty years later. She is a 'synthetic' composition, made up of recollections of the historical person of the mother of Jesus, New Testament legends and scriptural quotations from the Old Testament. Her portrait was painted in the image of age-old mother deities and virgin goddesses. The 'most pure virgin Mary' was begotten by theological speculation, pure longing of the heart and a sublimation of drives. She was born of faith and superstition, of the calculations of ecclesiastical power politics and the naive needs of popular piety. However, this 'Mary of faith' has little to do with the woman who gave birth to Jesus.

Sometimes I feel that if the historical Mary, the mother of Jesus, knew what people would make of her after her death, she would be very surprised and would completely fail to understand the spiritual servants of her son. If she had a sense of humour, was realistic and had a touch of curiosity, she might perhaps say with a laugh, 'You made it all up! You're joking. I'm not like that at all.' Or she could be annoyed and say grumpily, 'If for some reason you want to put together an idealized female figure, then please choose someone else, not me!'

'You mysterious rose'

'I see you in a thousand pictures, Mary, painted with love. But none can paint you as my soul sees you.' So sings Novalis, the poet of German Romanticism. Today I once again read through the Lauretian Litany and was touched by the beauty of the imagery with which Mary is praised in it: 'You mysterious rose, you cause of our joy, you venerable chalice, you golden house, holy mother of God, you mother intact, you wonderful mother, you wise virgin, you powerful virgin, you throne of wisdom, you gate of heaven, you morning star, you refuge of sinners, you comforter of the disturbed, you queen, taken up into heaven . . .'

Images have power. And I sense that something in me is ready to yield to the magic of these images and to succumb to their beauty, despite all critical rationality. If I see the words in which the church speaks of Mary as images which have been projected from the human soul to exalt the mother of Jesus, as images which symbolically express the longing of the human heart to revere the feminine, the maternal which gives security, the powerful one who helps, I can understand them. If I see these words as images which reflect the longing for the wholly good, the wholly pure, the wholly true, then I recognize that they refer to the figure of Jesus. Then I can even say yes to them.

I venerate Mary as the mother of Jesus.

14

'Like the grass which flourished in the morning'

Love which wants to survive death

We had just been to the funeral of a young man. He was around forty years old and had died in a car accident. His parents were friends of ours. The young man and his wife had left the church years before. We had respected this decision, because we knew that neither of them had taken this step lightly.

When we were leaving the cemetery after the burial, the wife came up to me, grasped me by the arm, and asked me urgently, 'Tell me, do you too believe that I shall see him again?' That was a question put to me by an emancipated and intelligent woman, who was not a believer but was seeking an affirmative answer when faced with the final parting from her husband. Her urgent question expressed the claim of a love which wants to survive the death of the loved one. Love also resists death in the mourning over the death of a loved one. It is unwilling to accept the separation brought by death and hopes to see the loved one again, hopes for a reunion.

I said to her, 'Yes, I too believe that.' What else could I have said to her at this moment? Can one maintain an ethic of object-ive, matter-of-fact truth in the face of love's cry for eternity? Should I have told her that I have doubts whether we shall see dead loved ones after our death?

The human hope to survive and to see loved ones after death is probably largely rooted in love's longing for eternity.

A question without an answer?

Hardly any thoughtful people have not asked themselves what comes after death, regardless of whether they are Christians, Muslims or Hindus; believers or unbelievers. This is not just a question for pious people; it is a universal human question, a question of all thinking people. It is not a matter of intellectual curiosity; it is an urgent existential question.

Time and again we are beset with perplexity, helplessness and a lack of answers when we confront death; when someone who is close to us is dying; when we bury the dead and have to say farewell to them; when we ourselves, having grown old or confronting a terminal illness, have to look death in the face. The many phrases which resound over the open graves are probably merely an expression of this helplessness.

Nowhere is the question of God and a world beyond more oppressive than on the hairline boundary which separates our life from the unknown which comes to us afterwards. And we have no absolutely certain answer to this question. Certain knowledge of what follows our death is withheld from us. From all of us, no matter what we believe.

Uncertainty

Anyone who says that death is the end will certainly be able to produce many convincing reasons for this conviction, and it will be impossible to refute such a claim rationally, with clear proofs. But also, it cannot be ruled out that things could be different. Uncertainty here constantly arises at times when death threatens. Only this morning I read in the newspaper that the seriously ill French President Mitterand, who – as far as I know – is not a believing Christian, sought out the philosopher Jean Guitton to talk to him 'about the other world'.

Those who say that they believe in a new life after death will also be able to give reasons for their faith, even good reasons which are to be taken seriously. But they too will not be able to present certain proofs which give us absolute assurance. We cannot arrive at the certainty of a changed existence beyond death in the form of assured knowledge. We can only hope and believe.

A twenty-five-year-old student of electronics whom I keep asking for help when I have trouble with my computer told me that he firmly believed in an ongoing life after death. When I asked him the reason for his certainty, he said, 'I couldn't bear this life otherwise.'

Hoimar von Ditfurth, the great expert and popularizer of modern science, to whom I owe much of my knowledge of the modern view of the world, said in his last interview shortly before his death that he would soon get an answer to all his questions (23/ 100). He said that, although by his own confession he did not belong to any religious community. That has kept me thinking.

'You die with all the animals'

'Don't be deceived! There is no return. You die with all the animals. And there is nothing afterwards,' says Bert Brecht. A bitter statement, without any illusions, which many people find it difficult to accept. Is that the truth about our death, about our life? I shall attempt to approach the question in a matter-of-fact and sober way.

Indeed! Whether we struggle against it or not, we share death with the animals and passing away with the plants. 'Like the grass which flourished in the morning, so we wither away.' Those are the words of Psalm 90. Death came into the world with the development of life; it is a child of evolution. Without death, life would not have been able to develop further, unfold and attain higher structures. Human beings would never have arisen without death.

The development of organic life on this earth begins with the asexual self-reproduction of very simple forms of life. Every generation is a precise copy of the previous one – apart from occasional mistakes, mutants. There is no further development, no adaptation to changed environmental circumstances. If these circumstances change, the whole species can perish.

However, the mutants occasionally give rise to variants in the hereditary endowment of the species which lead to improvements in the capacity of the species for survival, especially where a species develops the capacity to incorporate other living organisms – to be specific, to devour other living beings. The competition between the species makes one species a threat and also a destroyer of the life of another species: death is born. From then on life can survive only if it destroys other life. A cruel principle, which underlies the creation of a 'loving God'.

Asexual propagation by self-reproduction already opened up the way to the 'death of species'. At the beginning of individual death is the 'invention' of sexual procreation, sexuality. It mixes the hereditary endowments of different individuals in ever new combinations and variants and thus produces constantly new genres of life by means of selection; these are better adapted to changing circumstances and also make a higher structuring of life possible. Sexual multiplication became the real motive force of evolution. It drove the development of life forward to the human level. The further development of the species necessitated a limit to the life-span of its individual members. Death is the price of life! Just as we share life with the animals, so we also share death with them (cf. 4/ 480f.).

'For the fate of the sons of men and the fate of beasts is the same; as one dies, so dies the other', says the Old Testament in a quite sober and realistic way (Ecclesiastes 3.19).

Death – the consequence of sin?

In view of our present knowledge about the origin of life and death, which I have been able to sketch out here only in a very brief and simplistic way, the understanding of death which is still taught in the papal Catechism is highly dubious. There we read: 'The Church's Magisterium, as authentic interpreter of the affirmations of Scripture and Tradition, teaches that death entered the world on account of man's sin' (1/ no.1008).

We find the interpretation of death as a guilty breach between human beings and the deity in many primeval myths. It is a mythical interpretation. The biblical interpretation to which the church's magisterium appeals is woven into this mythical way of thinking. Like all human beings, human beings in biblical times, too, were questioning and perplexed when faced with the power of death which puts an end to everything. Who had given it such power? Where does it come from? Death was always felt as a power hostile to God, the source of life. So could death come from God? No, it had to have come from a breach with God, from a culpable alienation between human beings and God. Not God, but human sin had to have been the cause of death. And at the time the biblical authors could express this answer which had been found by the reflection of believers only in the form of myth: death came into the world because the first human beings, Adam and Eve, sinned in paradise.

Is it really an 'authentic' interpretation if the church's magisterium interprets a myth as a description of facts? I have good reason to doubt that.

The no to death

We have in common with the animals not only death, but also the powerful drive to life. And therefore we resist death. Animals already attempt to avoid it by developing an alert sensitivity to threats, rapid reactions which prompt flight, and speed. They disguise themselves through mimicry, gather together in herds, flocks and swarms, and warn one another. They have added armour and claws, teeth and poisonous fangs, and they use their weapons not only to get prey but also as dangerous instruments for defence. Their lives are shot through with defence against death, although they are not consciously aware of this. (However, I am not so certain whether nevertheless there are not the preliminary stages of a 'knowledge' of the threat of death among highly developed animals like chimpanzees, dolphins and perhaps also dogs; at least in the actual moment of threat.)

But it is probably reserved to human beings to *know* about death. Each of us knows that our own death is inevitable. And this knowledge gives rise to anxiety about death. We can suppress anxiety, but it keeps lurking in the background and breaks out when we encounter death. Anxiety about finally no longer being here has a secret and usually unconscious background influence on our hope to live on in our children, or in the works that we have done, or in the respectful memory of our fellow human beings, or even in posterity.

Living on after death?

The readiness to cling on to a hope in the face of the inevitability of death, which offers the prospect of nevertheless in some way avoiding the finality of death in a world beyond and of living on in some way, seems to be rooted deep in the hearts of most people.

So who can be surprised if notions of living on after death permeate the whole of human history, already beginning with the primeval cults of the dead and of ancestors which involve putting objects in the tomb for life in the world to come? The pyramids of the ancient Egyptians are monumental documents to faith in an ongoing life expressed in stone. The idea of a life after death appears in almost all religions which there have been and are on earth. The splendid temples, pagodas and cathedrals, wrested out of human poverty and misery, have been erected on the foundation of human anxiety about dying and the hope of a new, better life in a world to come.

Ernst Bloch, the philosopher who wrote a book called *The Principle of Hope*, said that the victory of Christianity over the pagan religions of antiquity was not due to the call of the Sermon on the Mount but to Christ's call, 'I am the resurrection and the life'. The quite concrete hope was that through baptism, like Jesus, one would not remain among the dead but rise with him to a new life (cf.13/ 65).

Dying into nothingness?

The notion of an ongoing life after death has never really played a specially important role in my own life of faith. Certainly I have accepted belief in an eternal life for myself along with the rest of Christian belief, and that is what I have taught. However, for me Christian faith, like the sacramental life of the church and moral behaviour, was never bound up with the expectation that as a result after my death I would share in an eternal life. In faith, too, my gaze was directed more towards life before death than towards 'life after death'. The basic orientation of the teaching and person of Jesus became a pointer for me to life on earth, and never a 'means towards attaining eternal bliss'.

So the possibility that with death it could finally be all over for me, that I would really die into nothingness and then never know anything about my own existence, did not oppress me particularly. I should then no longer feel any differently from the way I which I felt in the early Stone Age, in the time of the Pharaohs or Pericles, in the year in which Jesus was crucified, in the year 800 when Charlemagne was crowned, in the year 1756 when Mozart was born. I would sense nothing of myself and know nothing about myself: 'After your death,' says Schopenhauer, 'you will be as you were before your birth.'

I am less afraid of being dead than of the misery of dying, of tormenting illness, of lasting pain and humiliating dependency. I can hear a prayer which has been familiar since childhood and often spoken: 'May the Lord graciously preserve us from a sudden and unexpected death.' Today I would ask him to grant me a speedy death without long suffering. Once dead, I would no longer feel anything, no pain, no anxiety, no distress. There would be peace and rest, 'eternal rest'.

But the human heart longs for more. And it expects this 'more' from God: new life, changed life, eternal life.

Dying into everything?

Christian hope in a life beyond death is based on belief in the resurrection of Jesus. I found in Hans Küng an understanding of the resurrection of Jesus which helped me: 'Jesus did not die into nothingness, but in death and from death was taken into that incomprehensible and all-embracing last and first reality to which we give the name God' (13/148).

Resurrection means that Jesus died into a 'reality' which beyond space and time, beyond life and death, embraces, brings forth and supports the whole of the world, a reality which cannot be grasped, a reality which we usually imagine under the image of an active person and call 'God'. Jesus, faith says, did not die into nothingness but into everything, into the whole, into God. This dimension of 'eternity' is not a reality which is governed by a 'before' or 'after' death; it embraces the whole of space and time, of matter and spirit, of life and death.

But is there such a reality? We cannot prove it. I recall Hoimar von Ditfurth, who has always taught that reality does not end where our capacity for knowledge comes up against its limits. Especially the evolutionary history discovered by Konrad Lorenz makes one thing certain: '. . . the insight that the objectively existing world is not identical with what we experience as our reality' (21/ 383).

So is it 'reasonable', as Küng says, to trust that beyond the reality which we experience there is a new, greater, more comprehensive reality?

Dying into God

If there really were to be that last (and first) reality which brings forth, permeates, supports and embraces the whole of the world, the universe, and life on the globe, including my little life, that reality which we call 'God', then 'in a reasonable trust, in enlightened faith' I could also understand my own dying as a 'dying into God' and accept it (cf. 15/ 187).

If everything in this world is to experience its goal and its consummation in that last reality, then I can no longer close myself off to the hope that my own life could also experience its goal, its resolution, its liberation, its omega point there: God not just the origin of the whole, God also as its ultimate goal; God not just the source of all life, but also the ocean in which it issues. 'For from him and through him and to him are all things' (Rom.11.36).

If I trust in that, my personal death fits into the whole. It makes my death appear more than just a meaningless fate; it also links it to the meaning of the whole, to God. My existence is held fast by God. With all that is, I shall return into the living, all-embracing ground from which all things emerged.

A special human privilege?

It's now almost thirty years ago, but I still remember it very clearly. My daughter, who was then around ten years old, came home from school distraught and told us that she definitely didn't want to go to heaven. When I asked her in amazement why she didn't want to go to heaven, she told me that the teacher of religion had explained in a lesson that one day men and women would be able to live very near to God, together with many angels. 'Aren't there any animals in heaven, then?,' she asked. 'No,' she was told, 'animals can't go to heaven. They don't have immortal souls.' 'If there are no animals in heaven,' she then said to me, 'then I don't want to go to heaven either.'

No abiding in death, but resurrection, new life in a changed form, abiding bliss; those are the promises which the Christian tradition makes to believers. But does this promise apply only to human beings? I have never yet heard talk in church of a resurrection of chimpanzees, dogs, oxen or even toads and snakes. But yes, I did read such an idea once in one person – it was Eugene Drewermann in a little book on 'The Immortality of Animals' (5). For this little book alone I pay him my respects.

But to most believers shaped by traditional church thought and such theologians the notion of a 'resurrection of the animals to eternal life' will seem absurd. It will prompt spontaneous repudiation, if not indignation, and at the least produce uncomprehending, dismissive laughter. Most usually do not raise the question.

Nevertheless, I would ask whether the promise of eternal life is a human privilege. Is it a special endowment of that species which in the present form of development as *homo sapiens* has existed only for some hundreds of thousands of years, and which has developed by chance on a small globe from forms of life that today we classify as animals?

How far would we have to go back in the history of our species to be able to speak of a call of human beings to eternal life? To the Stone Age, or even to the Neanderthals, or say 1.6 million years further back to *homo erectus*, or say 2 million years back to *homo habilis*? Did the living being which some millions of years ago, somewhere on the margins of the Africa steppe, came down from the trees, learned to walk upright, used tools, and developed thought and language, share in the good fortune of being raised again after his death?

And where is the frontier, say, with *Australopithecus*

anamensis, who is nowadays regarded as the common ancestor of human beings and chimpanzees? It lived around four to five million years ago. Where is the frontier between animals and human beings which is decisive for immortality? I remember reading somewhere that we have 98.4 of our genes in common with the chimpanzees, our cousins. Are the ridiculously few 1.6 our own capital, which grant us an immortal soul and promise us a life beyond death?

Although it is indisputable that spirit, consciousness, thought and other capacities are most highly developed in human beings, today we can no longer start by assuming an absolute otherness of human beings from the other thirty million forms of life, as was still possible in former times. According to our present-day knowledge of the development of human beings, the frontier between human beings and animals cannot clearly be defined. The borderlines between species are blurred.

And we men and women of today are still beings in transition. So where should the frontiers of participation in the 'resurrection of the flesh' be put? Are there only a few links and some billions of neurones and synapses more in the brain which give us the hope of eternal life? Or is it the much-cited 'immortal soul' which has found its way into church doctrine from Greek philosophy? But there too one must ask from what stage of development an immortal soul can be promised to human beings.

. . . *thought of too anthropocentrically*

My guess is that the usual restriction of resurrection faith to human beings derives less from a 'divine revelation' than from an innate peculiarity of the brain, conditioned by development, to assimilate, evaluate and use reality almost exclusively from the perspective of our own species. The widespread religious view that only human beings are called to immortality as 'the image of God' may be rooted in an innate anthropocentricity of thought, of which those who think in this way are not even aware.

The excessive emphasis on the distinction between the human being endowed with an 'immortal soul' and animals 'without souls' is particularly widespread in the lands of the Mediterranean and the East, the lands in which the Christian religion had its origin. It has reinforced a lack of compassion and feeling towards animals and has become the cause of much torment and suffering.

My concern here is not to promise animals unconditionally a life after death; I am concerned with human beings. But if there is not to be a 'resurrection of the flesh' for the rest of creation, then it is hard to see today why it should await only human beings. If there were to be a life after death for human beings, then in our present knowledge of the place of human beings within the development of life, it is difficult to give convincing reasons for excluding the rest of life from it.

'They all have the same breath, and human beings have no precedence over animals.' Ecclesiastes already taught that in the Old Testament.

The consummation of all things?

If there really should be life beyond this earthly life, then this other reality of new perfect existence would have to be something for the whole of the world: not just for human beings, but also for animals and plants. This newly dawning reality would have to be the consummation and goal of everything in the world: from the elementary particles of matter to human beings.

The Bible in fact presents the vision of a 'new creation'. It talks of 'a new heaven and a new earth', in which everything finds its consummation and fulfilment. 'Behold, God will be with men and women. The old is past. And God said, "I make all things new"' (Rev.21.2-5).

The idea of evolution in the natural sciences, which sees the universe and life involved in a movement towards a future which is still open and unknown, matches this biblical vision, and at least helps us to understand its promise.

All too human notions

Does that then mean that I believe that after my personal death one day I shall have new *personal* life, though in quite a different way? Does it mean that I shall then be conscious of myself, that I will know that I am there, that I am alive, personally? Does it mean that I can hope there – I hope, in heaven – to see again my dead parents and the many loved ones whose funerals I have attended? Do I believe that I shall then be in a state of eternal bliss and will also experience this happiness personally? Do I believe that justice will then be restored, injustice recognized and lies unmasked?

I find it difficult, but here first of all I must honestly say 'No!'. I do not believe in an idea like *this*. And in saying no I think that I am in good company, indeed the best. Jesus himself opposed such naively realistic transferences of all too human expectations and notions to the resurrection. He rejected the question of the Sadducees, who asked to whom the wife of seven brothers who died one after the other would be married after the resurrection: 'You are in error, because you do not know scripture nor the power of God. For in the resurrection they do not marry, nor are they given in marriage' (Matt.22.29).

Our starting point must be that even our notions of a life after death are as inadequate as those of the Sadducees. These ideas are merely projections of what is important on earth on a world beyond. They are human, all too human, and also inappropriate. Resurrection does not mean any extension of our present life but a transition into a completely different dimension of reality.

Images of hope

Our capacity for imagination, which has developed over many hundreds of thousands of years under the conditions of space and time on the globe, has not produced any appropriate categories for the 'wholly other' reality which we term 'resurrection'. So we cannot imagine this 'wholly other' reality. It does in fact lie 'beyond' our capacity for imagining.

If we nevertheless speak of this hoped-for 'wholly other' reality, then we depend on images which derive from the world of our human experience. The very word 'resurrection' is such a image and does not describe a real process. It is an image for opening up a new dimension of reality which we cannot name.

Even the words with which the Bible attempts to express its hope that the creation will 'be in God' are images: 'God will dwell with them and they shall be his people, and God himself shall be with them; he will wipe away every tear from their eyes, and death shall be no more, neither shall there be mourning nor crying nor pain any more' (Rev.21.34f.). It is a marvellous picture which promises us what we long for: no more pain, no more misery, no more hunger, no more sickness, no more disputes, no alienation, no hatred, no more cruel wars, no more meaningless suffering of creation; only peace, joy, happiness and love.

We also know the image of the heavenly marriage feast, the image of the heavenly Jerusalem, the image of the Last Judgment, a final putting right, the image of the glory of heaven. These are all images which arise from the unquenchable longing of the human heart for fulfilment, for abiding happiness; the longing for liberation from all that torments us in this life . . . They are images of hope, paintings of longing, visions of a hoped-for fulfilment.

The dark counterpart of heaven, hell, painted on a negative background, is also a projection of human expectations. It derives from a human nature which cannot be content that injustice should remain unatoned-for for ever, that those who in their wickedness have brought infinitely much suffering upon others should fare in the same way as their innocent victims. The flames of hell are kindled in the human heart.

We fill the unimaginable reality beyond the frontier of death with imaginable content; we cannot do otherwise. So should these images be rejected?

Painted by human expectations

The pictures in which hope paints the coming fulfilment are of human origin. They are projections from the world of human experience, drawn differently, depending on the horizon, the needs, of different cultures.

Hindus paint a picture of peace in which greed, hatred and blindness are no more and all suffering has found an end. Indians ride through the eternal hunting grounds. The Islamic Qur'an colours the beyond in the strong hues of earthly joys: in the midst of gardens with clear streams the righteous rest on couches adorned with precious stones. Houris, beautiful young women, serve them with precious food, costly wine and mead, and also accustom them to the joys of love (cf. 12/238).

The pictures painted by Christian theologians are less sensual. They see eternal happiness above all in a 'beatific vision', a 'blissful vision of God'. In the Christian heaven there is nothing to eat, no wine to drink, and there are no sensual joys; no life of love, no animals and no plants, but many saints with haloes and angels to sing alleluia. I would prefer to be in the Muslim paradise!

But I would also be pleased to be in the world which the prophets of the Old Testament paint for us: 'The wolf shall dwell with the lamb, and the leopard shall lie down with the kid, and the calf and the lion and the fatling together, and a little child shall lead them. The cow and the bear shall feed; their young shall lie down together; and the lion shall eat straw like the ox; the sucking child shall play over the hole of the asp, and the weaned child shall put his hand on the adder's den. They shall not hurt or destroy in all my holy mountain' (Isa.11.6-9).

Certainly, they are all pictures which have been painted from the hopes and expectations of earthly human beings. But perhaps in these pictures there already gleams the light of a reality which, while it is quite different, is nevertheless there and waiting for us: the world of God.

Personal survival?

Of course I don't know. Who could know? But I think that the notion of a personal survival after death is simply a picture which, while it is certainly vivid and indeed beautiful, is still only a picture like the many others through which we human beings fill the unimaginable with imaginable content and elaborate it in order to describe the indescribable. Like all other pictures, this one too derives from our human world of experience.

So we cannot do other than imagine an existence after death, too, as a personal life, with personal identity, with personal awareness of ourselves, with personal thought and action and happiness which we experience personally. This is perhaps the only picture with which human beings can imagine an existence in a reality which will open up to them in the future. I can therefore calmly accept this picture of a personal life after death for myself also. But I have to remember that reality is different from the picture that we paint in accordance with our earthly and human notions.

'For now we see in a mirror dimly, but then face to face. Now I know in part; then I shall understand fully, even as I have been fully understood.' That's how Paul puts it.

No more doubt

After so much critical and 'enlightened' reflection, perhaps at the end I may be allowed for once, in quite a naive way, in what is perhaps is a post-critical second naivety, to paint a quite personal picture of my hope.

If what we call God really should be there, then I am certain that one day I shall come to him. He will not turn away someone who has sought him all his life; not even if he has often gone astray and made many mistakes.

And if I may also be allowed to imagine my God in an equally naive way as a friendly person, who is waiting for me somewhere in the land beyond my death, perhaps at a wedding feast, then I imagine that he will say to me: 'I'm glad that you've found your way to me at last. I've seen how you've always been looking for me. You've taken some unnecessary detours. You could have done it more easily. You look tired. Now come, sit down and drink a glass of wine with me.' Yes, then I shall rejoice and be happy. Then perhaps there will no longer be any doubt.

A beautiful picture, but still only a picture. Perhaps more, though: a little creed which may not remove the doubts that trouble me, but does embrace them. Until I see Him 'face to face', things will probably go on as they do now. I believe, I doubt.

Bibliography

of books referred to or quoted from

1. *Catechism of the Catholic Church*, London 1994
2. Rolf Baumann and Helmut Haug (eds.), *Thema Gott*, Stuttgart 1970
3. Eugen Drewermann, *Giordano Bruno*, Munich 1992
4. – , *Glauben in Freiheit, Dogma, Angst und Symbolismus*, Solothurn 1993
5. – , *Über die Unsterblichkeit der Tiere*, Olten and Freiburg 1990
6. Irenäus Eibl-Eibesfeldt, *Der Mensch – das riskierte Wesen*, Munich 1988
7. Karlheinz Deschner, *Abermals krähte der Hahn*, Rastatt 1990
8. Mircea Eliade, *A History of Religious Ideas*, Chicago 1979
9. H.Haag and E.Drewermann, *Lasst Euch die Freiheit nicht nehmen*, Zurich 1993
10. Stephen W.Hawking, *A Brief History of Time*, London and New York 1988
11. *Katholischer Katechismus für die Bistümer Deutschlands*, 1955.
12. Hans Küng, *Credo*, London and New York 1993
13. – , *Eternal Life*, London and New York 1984
14. – , *Mozart. Traces of Transcendence*, London and Grand Rapids 1992
15. – , *Denkwege*, Munich 1992
16. Karl Lehmann, *Jesus Christus ist auferstanden*, Freiburg 1975
17. Uta Ranke-Heinemann, *Nein und Amen*, Hamburg 1992
18. Rupert Riedl, *Kultur – Spätzündung der Evolution*, Munich 1987
19. Schalom Ben Chorin, *Bruder Jesus*, Munich 1987
20. Hoimar von Ditfurth, *Unbegreifliche Realität*, Hamburg 1987
21. – , *Innenansichten eines Artgenossen*, Düsseldorf 1989

22. –, *Der Geist fiel nicht vom Himmel*, Hamburg 1976
23. – , and Dieter Zilligen, *Das Gespräch*, Düsseldorf 1990
24. H.von Mendelsohn, *Jesus, Rebell oder Erlöser?*, Munich 1987
25. A.N.Wilson, *Jesus*, London and New York 1993

In the references in the text, the number before the slash relates to the number of the title in this Bibliography, and the number after it to the page number. However, in the Catechism (1), the reference is to the section number.